BEYOND THE

SURFACE

*Navigating Human Resources
with Compassion and Insight*

ANGELA RASHEED-STEPHENS

Cover design by & Interior layout by Breakthrough Media Group

Printed in the United States of America

Published by: Self-Published by Angela Rasheed-Stephens

For permissions, bulk orders, or speaking engagements, contact:angie@premiersolitionsforlife.com or **linkedin.com/in/angiethelifecoach**

DEDICATION

This book, *Beyond the Surface: Navigating Human Resources with Compassion and Insight,* is a living record of a journey whose course was shaped through every twist, together with the love, wisdom, and unwavering help that remarkable individuals provided for me. I've never been able, after all, without everyone here, to say a big thank-you to them at once. This book is for all of us.

First, I want to thank my mom, Claudette Lamar. Mom, you are my anchor in the storm, the light that guides me through darkness. Early on, your love, powerful yet delicate, taught me how to see past the surface to inner beauty. Your example of social kindness isn't something we do; it is who we are. This is what you live every day: the truth expressed with serenity and compassion. Whenever my strength faltered or I felt lost, the melody of your voice was like a soft wind blowing in my ear. For just those small moments, it would be enough to make me keep on going. Compassion is the very heart of meaningful work. However, your guidance has broken through the reliance on external appearances that had long made me blind. Every one of your teachings I carry within me today, and they breathe life into every page of this book.

I am and always will be grateful for my pastor, Roger Obregon. Pastor, you opened my eyes to love in its purest form - agape love - love which calls upon us to see people as God does: with inexhaustible patience, dignity, and grace when it can take one a step of faith deeper than how others look at us. Your example of living that truth showed me how to bring faith and humility into my work. You taught me not only to judge by external actions, for you are always looking beyond them and meeting each person with an open heart, apart. This deeply influenced the very substance of this book, writings, and for it, I am deeply grateful.

Dr. Mechelle Garrett, thanks for never letting me stop wanting more out of life. When I was lost about my future, you urged me to keep researching. In the end, that gave me some emotion crossing paths again and again. You reminded me that learning is not an end in itself, but a lifelong search for new and growing gracefully alongside life. When I began to falter, your faith in me was like a firm hand guiding me on. I am so blessed, not only for the mentorship of Dr. Mechelle Garrett, but also because she sets such an inspiring example: a dedicated and fearless leader who sincerely seeks to help others rise up. For that, I am even more grateful.

Dr. Brenda Henton, thank you from the bottom of my heart for your generosity in helping me find my own voice. Your patience, love, and gentle persuasion opened up a space where I could be susceptible to others-where it mattered most was true to size, real ways have changed since then. You did not judge me, listened, and then gave me all the time I needed to see this through. You made it possible for me to be sure of myself through every confession. Because of you, this book isn't just a collection of experiences; rather, it's a form of relief. You've helped me turn personal pain into hope and strength for everyone who, in any way, has been broken by work trauma.

To you, Omar Ried, your leadership and your kindness have had an impact on me that words cannot fully convey. You knew me when I was a diamond in the rough, still trying to find my way and not really sure of my worth. You made it all right for me to fail, to stumble, to grow; yet you never left my side. With your courage, love, and example, you taught me what genuine leadership is supposed to be: not about gaining and using power but rather serving and doing no harm. You told me that truly great leaders enable others to shine, and you gave me the strength to find and use my own voice. Thank you for being both a mentor and a role model; above all, you are a true friend. I could never have made it this far without your support.

My gratitude is bottomless to my loved ones and dearest friends who held me up in times of self-doubt. You cheered me when I was down and savored every one of my small victories as though it were a major triumph. With your kindness, patience, and faith, you provided an anchor for every leap into the unknown that I made. I am infinitely grateful to have you standing in my corner.

This book is dedicated to all of these people, as well as every person who believes in the power of kindness, mutual understanding, and genuine human connection at work. I hope most deeply that these pages find their way into the hands not only of professionals and managers but also every employee who walks through the door of his or her workplace with unseen struggles. May it remind us all that behind each title, each role, each task we perform, there is a person-a human being who has fears, dreams, and a story worth hearing. But I beg you to bear this in mind: compassion and grace are not rules. They are the lifelines connecting individuals, the medicine that turns a job from a mere living into a fulfilled life. Thank you for walking this road with me. As these words go out into the world, each of you goes with me, and I hope they encourage you to show not just as an employee, but as people, imperfect, trying to better themselves, and worthy of some charity.

BEYOND THE SURFACE

TABLE OF CONTENTS

BEYOND THE SURFACE

FOREWORD

If you haven't noticed, our world is changing, and fast. The past five years alone have brought seismic shifts in how we live, work, and relate to one another. Looking ahead, the pace of change shows no signs of slowing down. Emerging technologies like generative and adaptive AI are reshaping not just our tools but the very fabric of workplace culture, demographics, and identity. As these new realities unfold, leaders, particularly those in Human Resources, must be prepared to navigate uncharted territory with wisdom, agility, and purpose.

I met Angie over thirty years ago, when we were both working in Human Resources at a Fortune 50 company. From the moment she walked into my office, I knew she was someone to watch. Her passion for people was evident from our very first conversation. She expressed a desire to join my team, even though I had no openings at the time. Still, I knew she would be my next hire. And when the opportunity finally came, bringing her on board became one of the best hiring decisions of my career.

Angie quickly proved to be a standout performer, consistently exceeding expectations and taking on multiple leadership roles with grace and skill. When I moved from the private sector into municipal government, Angie soon followed. Her leadership was instrumental in transforming a large, bureaucratic department into one that earned awards and became a model for others. Later, when I transitioned into the healthcare sector, she once again made the pivot, demonstrating not just loyalty but also the versatility and courage to lead in complex, evolving environments.

Over the years, I've watched Angie evolve from a promising leader into a true thought leader. Her depth of knowledge, curiosity, and relentless pursuit of meaningful change continue to inspire those around her.

This book is a powerful extension of her journey and her voice. It challenges us to think critically, lead boldly, and stay grounded in the values that matter most. If you're looking for practical insight, thoughtful perspective, and inspiration for growth, both personal and organizational, you'll find it here.

Prepare to be challenged. Prepare to grow. Angie has something important to say, and we would all do well to listen.

Omar Reid, MBA, IPMA-CP
Executive Vice President, Chief People Officer

Foreword

'When I think about human resources (HR), I realize how profoundly my perspective has evolved over the years. Early in my career, I viewed HR as an appendage to a company or organization. Necessary, but not central to day-to-day operations. HR was simply the department responsible for hiring, firing, and benefits, and the place you went to report a creepy boss or colleague. Over time and through experience, I've come to see HR as a powerful ally, partner, and resource in the workplace.

There were moments in my leadership journey when I faced challenging situations, including an underperforming employee, workplace stress, difficult conversations with colleagues or employees, or fractured team relationships. Not knowing what to do or the best course of action, I turned to HR, and I'm glad I did. The HR representatives in those situations didn't lecture me about policy, rules, or laws. They helped me step back and see the situation as a whole rather than in parts. They brought perspective and understanding, helping me see the people behind the problems.

And when I walked through my own season of burnout, it was the HR team that gently stepped in and guided me through the process of taking care of myself. Burnout hit me hard, and I needed to step away from my role for an extended period of time. I was unsure how to begin navigating time off and what that could look like. I went to HR. The ladies' initial responses were empathy, concern, and understanding, not policies, processes, and procedures. Then, they guided me through the process of taking time off. I felt the heaviness of burnout begin to lift just sitting with them and knowing that they cared for and about me. I took five weeks off work during that time. HR was there for and with me during my time off and after my return to work.

When I share that story with other people, they are surprised by the way the HR department cared for and supported me. I realized that that is not everyone's experience with HR. After all, it hadn't always been mine. So, when Angie told me she was writing a book about her experiences as a leader in HR and her vision for the field and its professionals, I became excited. This book is needed. Her vision is needed. Her ideals and passion for serving others in this capacity are needed. The knowledge Angie shares regarding HR, leadership, and employees will help transform the workplace and reshape organizational cultures. I hope it will help others have positive experiences with their HR departments, colleagues, and employees.

I've known Angie for nearly 25 years. The values she shares in this book are dear to her and are lived out in her own life and profession. Angie has nearly 30 years of experience in human resources, and she brings not just experience and expertise, but passion and care, to every chapter of this book. She tells the truth about the challenges, but she also paints a picture of what's possible when HR is empowered to lead with empathy and concern, as well as structure and policy.

Angie reminds us that human resources is not a department. It is a commitment. A commitment to see, to understand, and to care for the human being behind the employee number. Angie reminds us, or perhaps shows us, that HR, when done right, is not just part of the organization-it is the heart of it.

Whether you're in HR, managing a team, or simply an employee, you need the insights found in these pages. From the invisible struggles of toxic leadership to the silent crises employees bring to the workplace each day, this book is both a diagnosis and a remedy. Because great workplaces don't happen by accident, they are shaped by people who care enough to do the hard work of listening, confronting, and building trust.

Mechelle Garrett, Ed.D.
Higher Education Executive Leader

CHAPTER 1
INTRODUCTION

The story unfolds as a tale of an employee suspended for a seemingly trivial offense: misuse of a cell phone. My mind raced back to when an organization teetered between decentralization and centralization. The power struggles were palpable, the old guard clinging to their fiefdoms, their humanity buried beneath layers of policy manuals. The employee's name, lost to anonymity, was etched in my memory. She had been sent home, her fate sealed by a few keystrokes. But what lay beneath the surface? Why had she risked her job for a forbidden call or text? This was the question I asked myself. As I grappled with the question, I had to understand how this happened.

Many years ago, I worked at an organization that was in the process of moving from a decentralized structure (where every entity also had its human resources (HR) professionals and where the departments managed each function, i.e., "each man to his tent") towards migration into centralization that involved one unified team for human resources concerns across various aspects related to workforce management. This was intended to simplify operations and bring greater efficiency.

The shift from personnel to a more centralized process-driven approach led to significant power struggles that drew attention to wrong processes and ineffective decision-making. Departments used to make their own decisions independently now had to navigate a new, centralized HR system. The organization was stuck seeing HR as personnel. They didn't understand that HR had transformed from an administrative function to a dynamic and integral part of organizational strategy and success.

This was compounded by the fact that, in most cases, employees of the previous HR teams had become accustomed to the decentralized structure and resisted the new centralized processes. They would frequently circumvent established procedures to reach premature conclusions. This power struggle crippled operations as the HR team mainly consisted of administrative professionals working low on the organization chart and were helpless against others higher up. The HR structure was stuck in the tradition of how things had previously operated, and employees were afraid to make decisions. Human Resources became a place where personal development was stifled, and every decision required the approval of the next level, so this was a vicious cycle that sought only to reduce the issue at hand from the HR professional's perception that they existed solely to make the problem disappear.

One day, I got a call that would forever change everything. I received a call from one of the department heads who told me he had been contacted by information technology (IT) in the previous month concerning an employee who they thought was abusing her company phone. Many organizations routinely check for suspicious or unauthorized traffic entering and exiting the network. Red flags would go up whenever traffic patterns on the network pointed to any websites that were not allowed, even if it was from an employee's cell phone. They may also use security software that scans for malware or inappropriate content. IT told the department that a flagged website had been visited using a cell.

The centralized (new) HR was not informed of this then. Instead, the department chose to look into the inquiry itself. I found out later that the investigation was simple - reviewing documented information from the IT staff, checking policies, and confronting the employee about what happened. The employee denied the allegation but was not heard because the person investigating the claim saw this employee as someone with privilege. The perception was that the employee would often come in late or miss work and would never be held accountable for her actions since she worked for an executive. The individual who conducted the investigation had a built-in bias, and at the end of the so-called investigation, the decision was made to suspend the employee.

The initial investigation was flawed as it did not investigate its proper depths; It lacked empathy and failed to identify precisely where the infraction started. Anytime HR investigates workplace matters, the layers should be peeled to determine what happened. Doing right by employees and practicing empathy means providing safe spaces for open conversation. This approach ensures fairness. Organizations have two tools: sensitivity and active listening. During an investigation, it is essential not only to hear the words spoken but also to listen to the unspoken things. By doing so, HR can find the root cause of the issue.

HR professionals play a pivotal role in the complex landscape of organizational policies. However, rigid adherence to policies can sometimes backfire. Organizations often enforce policies without considering the unique context or individual circumstances. While policies provide structure and consistency, they may only cover some scenarios. Blindly following them can hinder adaptability and creative problem-solving.

A rigid adherence to a policy may result in unfavorable outcomes. HR professionals should recognize that flexibility is essential to address complexity effectively. Employee Relations is NEVER black and white. Consistency is vital, but it shouldn't come at the cost of adaptability. HR professionals should interpret policies contextually, considering factors like an employee's history. Sometimes, deviating from policy is necessary for fairness and practicality. HR professionals must look beyond surface-level behaviors (e.g., rule violations) and address the root cause of the issue.

Remember, HR professionals are the bridge between policy and people. Their ability to balance rigidity with empathy and adaptability ensures a healthier workplace. After the department leader informed me of the infraction, he told me the employee had passed away. The news was devastating, and the department needed immediate assistance from HR to manage the crisis.

As I hung up the phone, it rang again. And again. Soon, I was flooded with calls from employees and leaders, demanding to know how this could have happened and why HR hadn't intervened sooner. My priority was to provide support to the grieving department. I quickly arranged for our Employee Assistance Program (EAP) to step in and offer counseling and support. But it was clear that there were deeper issues at play. We needed to understand why the previous concerns raised by employees about this particular employee had not been escalated to central HR and addressed.

The first HR team believed they had the authority to decide what issues needed to be reported to central HR, further exacerbating the breakdown in communication and oversight. The mishandling of the initial investigation reflected this systemic failure. The old guard strictly adhered to their outdated protocols, prioritizing bureaucratic procedures over human empathy. Reports of concerns about the employee were not escalated because they didn't fit neatly into predefined categories or the way things had ALWAYS been done. The leaders believed they could decide what must be reported to central HR. This rigid adherence to policy and power struggles contributed to the failure, preventing a deeper understanding of the situation.

The initial investigation lacked empathy and failed to recognize the underlying issues. It was conducted in a cold, procedural manner, focusing on surface-level behaviors and infractions without considering the broader context of the situation. This approach alienated employees and missed critical warning signs that could have prompted timely intervention.

A new investigation by the central HR team revealed the critical importance of understanding the human element in HR practices. Rigid adherence to policy and power struggles can be detrimental in complex situations. HR professionals must look beyond surface-level behaviors and infractions to understand the underlying issues and context. This approach requires empathy, discernment, and a willingness to adapt policies to meet the needs of the people involved.

The secondary investigation team took a markedly different approach. They prioritized empathy and thoroughness, ensuring they fully understood the context of the situation. They conducted in-depth interviews with employees, actively listening to their concerns and experiences. This empathetic approach led to the discovery of critical information that had been overlooked initially. Through careful investigation, it was uncovered that the employee had been dealing with domestic abuse, a fact that the initial investigation had missed entirely. This understanding brought to light the severe stress and fear she was under, explaining many of her behaviors that were previously dismissed as mere infractions. It was later determined that the abuser had possession of the phone.

The contrasting outcomes of the two investigations provided valuable lessons for HR professionals. The initial investigation's failure highlighted the dangers of a rigid, procedural approach that lacks empathy and understanding. The secondary investigation demonstrated the importance of compassion, discernment, and context in HR practices. By focusing on the human element and actively listening to employees, HR professionals can better support their workforce and address underlying issues before they escalate.

The tragic incident involving this employee underscored the importance of empathy and understanding in HR practices. The initial procedural approach, focused on policy adherence rather than holistic understanding, missed crucial details about her situation, contributing to a devastating outcome. However, the subsequent investigation, which prioritized empathy and thoroughness, uncovered deeper issues like domestic abuse that had gone unnoticed.

The lessons learned highlight the critical need for HR to adapt policies with empathy and flexibility, especially in complex and sensitive situations. Clear communication, robust reporting mechanisms, and a supportive workplace culture emerged as essential pillars in navigating crises and ensuring the well-being of employees.

Organizations can balance policy adherence with a compassionate approach to well-being by creating a thoughtful, integrated strategy that includes transparent and flexible policies, creating a supportive culture, and ensuring all employees are provided with the appropriate resources and training. It's also important to note that policies should be reviewed, updated regularly, and balanced with support from discipline.

The following insights highlight crucial issues regarding employee support, burnout, and the effects of organizational changes. Understanding these aspects is vital for ensuring employee well-being and productivity. The declining support for organizational changes signals a growing sense of change fatigue among employees, which can obstruct the successful implementation of new policies. Effective change management, clear communication, and support systems are essential to mitigate burnout and improve the acceptance of changes.

Some important statistics to consider from various sources:

- Employees are three times as likely to explore their options if they don't feel supported.
- If employees feel stable in their careers, they're 20% more likely to still work at their current company in a year.
- 75% of employees experience burnout.
- Around 40% of workers said they've experienced burnout during the pandemic, perhaps because 37% of employees work longer hours.
- Burnout also seems to trend more toward women, with 43% of female leaders experiencing burnout compared to 31% of male leaders.
- 45% of employees are burned out by organizational changes in 2023.
- Back in 2016, 74% of employees were willing to support organizational changes, but that number dropped to 38% in 2022. That's likely why, for 53% of HR leaders, mitigating this change fatigue is a top priority.
- 30% of new hires leave within 90 days.
- The reasons employees leave aren't a shocker: 43% say the role doesn't meet their expectations, 34% leave because of a specific incident, and 32% don't think the company culture is a good fit.
- Creating a supportive and adaptable work environment is crucial. Addressing what makes employees unhappy or likely to leave can lead to a more engaged, productive, and loyal workforce. Organizations can build a thriving workplace by

focusing on employee well-being, managing changes effectively, and improving onboarding and company culture.

This book is for all of us. It is essential to understand that at any stage of our career, we are just people trying to do our job in the best possible way. It is easy for employees and those in leadership to get very caught up in their roles, forgetting that we are all human people with our struggles and dreams. We all have weaknesses and flaws, and everyone has obstacles and triumphs. This realization can prompt a more compassionate working environment. It is easy to place blame, but showing empathy takes work and understanding. Instead of constantly complaining about the boss or company (I hear this every day), find a way out. Think about what you are adding to the mix. Are you adding value? Are you helping to build a culture of positivity and productivity?

When you focus on your input, you're claiming responsibility for your end of the workplace relationship. This could mean searching (within yourself) for what changes might help. Can you give your colleague a boost? Do you have a solution mindset? How do you face problems? In the grand scheme of things, little shifts can have significant results over time. By focusing on what you can control, you move from a mindset of victimhood to one of responsibility and empowerment. It does not mean that we should overlook festering issues, but it is about how you will engage in the process of bringing a resolution to such matters. We are empowered to help instigate organizational change by owning our part. It sounds overly simplistic; however, creating a better place of work starts with everyone individually. Together, when we all do our best and help each other succeed, we foster a more collaborative and supportive atmosphere. Developing an entrepreneurial mindset increases morale, productivity, and job satisfaction.

To sum it up, this book reminds us that we share the same responsibility. When what you think, say, and do align with higher thoughts of good, gratefulness, and service, you help yourself enjoy your life more each day and brighten the skies for those in your sphere. YOU are the CHANGE you want to see.

CHAPTER 2
The Human Element: Recognizing Our Greatest Asset Beyond Policy

At the heart of every strategic endeavor lies a profound truth: the most invaluable asset of any organization is its people. Consequently, businesses must pivot their focus to prioritize the well-being and growth of their team members. This entails a fundamental shift where strategy, development, and innovation converge to nurture individual flourishing. Essential to this transformation is cultivating a culture of trust, transparency, and open communication guided by empathetic and insightful leadership. A clear strategic roadmap becomes indispensable, steering leaders and employees toward shared objectives. Investing in leadership development is crucial to equip those leading teams with the requisite skills and empathy.

In an organization's dynamic world, becoming ensnared in numbers and protocols is too easy. However, at its core, human resources revolves around people. The human element isn't merely a strategy component-it is essential to shaping a thriving workplace. This chapter underscores the significance of the human element as the cornerstone for establishing a vibrant and supportive work environment. It encompasses the intricacies of the behaviors, motivations, and aspirations of individuals. In an era increasingly dominated by impersonal resumes, the essential humanity of our colleagues often fades from view. We must introspect: where does the 'human being' stand within our companies today? Are employees relegated to mere cogs in the corporate machinery? This approach breeds discontent and overlooks a fundamental truth: businesses are constructed by people, for people.

The ramifications of this oversight extend beyond the personal realm; they resonate within the realms of economics and society. People are the driving force behind economic progress, yet within the confines of corporations, they're frequently reduced to mere entries on a spreadsheet, an impersonal statistic. We urgently require a shift in perspective within companies regarding their most precious asset: their people. It's time to regard employees not merely as numbers but as individuals endowed with unique strengths and aspirations. The imperative for 'human being' processes, approaches that authentically acknowledge and harness all individuals' diverse capabilities and aspirations, has never been more pressing. This shift transcends mere enhancement of job satisfaction; it's about unleashing the full potential of our workforce. Companies must begin to recognize their employees as human beings, not just numerical entities. We necessitate systems that appreciate the multifaceted nature of our workforce, particularly those who thrive on being more than just another cog in the wheel.

At this pivotal juncture, businesses must grasp that their paramount asset resides in their human capital. The future of work hinges on our capacity to identify and nurture our workforce's varied talents and passions. It's time to transition from a transactional to a transformational approach in how we perceive our employees. Companies should embrace more human-centric processes, where understanding an employee's true essence, potential, and satisfaction is as paramount as evaluating their qualifications and experience.

The solution commences with a fundamental shift in how we perceive and esteem our employees. The focus must transcend mere job fulfillment to genuinely comprehend and leverage the human potential within our organizations. It entails cultivating environments where our workforce discovers employment and a platform to exercise their innate abilities, construct, innovate, and find fulfillment. For companies to flourish, they must do more than merely attract talent; they must engage, understand, and nurture it. This necessitates reimagining recruitment and retention strategies to prioritize the holistic individual rather than simply fulfilling job description prerequisites. By recognizing what an individual has accomplished and can achieve, businesses can elevate employee satisfaction and unlock new thresholds of innovation and productivity.

I previously discussed the significance of establishing a culture centered on trust, transparency, and open communication, guided by empathetic and insightful leadership. Let's delve further into this concept. Modern employees have heightened expectations, seeking fair compensation, a positive work environment, autonomy, respect, and opportunities to showcase their abilities. Organizations must transition from simply engaging employees to authentically fostering a people-centric culture that aligns with individuals' preferred workstyles and motivates them to excel. This type of culture emphasizes purpose and significance. In less developed organizations, managers often perceive employees conventionally, assigning them predefined roles within a hierarchical structure along with specific tasks and duties. This outdated method can result in disengagement. Consequently, while the talent acquisition team concentrates on external recruitment, the organization overlooks nurturing its current staff members who may benefit from additional training to enter new positions. Unsurprisingly, many employees find existing workforce management procedures unproductive in enhancing their job performance. Conversely, mature organizations prioritize their employees' success by continuously evaluating the overall employee experience instead of merely assessing tasks and key performance indicators (KPIs) against a checklist. The goal is to bolster the employee brand, retain current talent, and attract new skilled professionals. This holistic approach fosters an environment where employees feel appreciated and encouraged to contribute meaningfully to the organization's achievements. Organizations can cultivate a dynamic and driven workforce prepared to confront today's competitive landscape by concentrating on employee development and well-being. Transitioning towards a more mature and empathetic organizational culture will lead to sustained success and expansion. By employee development, I do not mean just the routine training that any organization is accountable for. I mean helping employees explore what they are passionate about and discover where their actual skills lie. It is about putting in time to determine what strengths and interests each employee has and then figuring out what we can do to support them. Most employees have abilities not reflected in their daily chores, and identifying these capabilities would benefit both the employee and the organization.

The employee development process entails unlocking these hidden skills and providing pathways for employees to flourish in the areas that interest them. Workers who are interested and good at their work also have an easier time being engaged and motivated. This method increases their job satisfaction and how much they get done overall. By helping employees cultivate individual talents, organizations can make a tangible difference in their prospects for success. By empowering employees to deploy those hidden strengths, they contribute a new level of originality in their roles. Not only does this increase their productivity, but it can also positively affect the team and company.

However, utilizing these hidden skills in the company can contribute hugely to a positive company culture. For example, they can help inspire an employee to take initiative in a particular area that interests them and drive new initiatives or better processes, preventing downstream issues that would cause your organization to be less efficient and effective. The focus on uncovering hidden skills and developing them can be a potent employee development approach for organizations. With proper cause (i.e., specialized interests), we can let employees work on what they love, which will drive higher engagement, increased productivity, and overall success for the business! Such an approach benefits the individual and the organization at large by letting it spread by one and getting it taken up and used elsewhere.

In today's evolving workplace scenario, leaders strive to establish hybrid and flexible work arrangements, create inclusive atmospheres, and devise robust development strategies for their teams. Transparency in decision-making is a key element often overlooked in the workplace. Employees value being informed and understanding their role within the organization. Research from Slack underscores this, revealing that more than 80% of employees desire a clearer understanding of how decisions are reached. Additionally, 87% of job seekers prioritize transparency in prospective workplaces, indicating a strong preference for openness and inclusion in decision-making processes. Establishing transparency fosters trust, which is essential for accountability, performance, and innovation. When employees have faith in leadership and comprehend expectations, they exhibit higher dedication to their roles. Understanding how their responsibilities contribute to the company's mission and success further enhances motivation. Studies cited in the Harvard Business Review indicate that individuals working in environments built on trust are significantly more engaged (76%) and satisfied with their work (29%).

Creating a transparent culture necessitates a proactive approach toward organizational direction. Firstly, offering clear development pathways to employees is crucial as it provides visibility into advancement opportunities. Clarity on promotion criteria aligned with individual growth plans demonstrates a commitment to employee progression. Secondly, aligning business objectives with goals promotes transparency by helping staff understand performance expectations and goal impacts. Despite this importance, research indicates that only 40% of employees feel clear about their company's strategies and objectives, leaving room for improvement. Lastly, effective communication and feedback mechanisms are pivotal to transparency efforts, starting from leadership to ensure organizational alignment. Business leaders should adopt a culture of transparency within their organizations as a fundamental practice and actively participate in it. Modern employees seek explanations behind tasks rather than instructions, marking a crucial shift many executives must make. In 2013, the Edelman Trust Barometer revealed that 82% of employees did not trust their superiors to be truthful. Although there has been some improvement since then, fewer than half of today's employees express trust in their bosses. Distrust can stem from inadequate communication, ambiguous objectives, or a failure to acknowledge mistakes. These flawed managerial approaches foster skepticism and cynicism among employees, especially when they witness inconsistencies such as favoritism or neglect towards underperformers.

As a leader, when you pick favorites or overlook poor performance by one person, everyone on the team notices the situation more than is apparent to you. These management blind spots lead to team members feeling frustrated, skeptical, and eventually cynical about the boss. People no longer talk about this sort of thing in passing only; it becomes a permanent undercurrent to discussions in the workplace. They bring it to how they dress, their tone, and how much it makes them feel that leadership is ahead of them, like road-crusty gravel.

A leader may dismiss it as "This is my pro-person, or go-to person," not knowing that the rest of the group will see things differently. In their eyes, it looks like special treatment, one person held to different standards while others strain against a heavy yoke of expectation. When an underperforming or disruptive employee goes unchallenged, the rest of the team picks up the bill. They are overworked, undervalued, and, at last, disengaged.

The results are profound. Employees begin to feel that what they do doesn't count, that there's no such thing as fairness anymore. Morale slips, cooperation frays, bitterness grows. In the end, talented people leave, not because they don't love work, but because their efforts are unappreciated and met with silence. For leaders, too, the damage is genuine. Trust vanishes, authority wanes, and what was once a laborious, engaged team becomes fragmented. The shocking part is that the leader is completely oblivious.

Good leadership is about more than just achieving results; it also entails fairness, equality, and seeing how actions (or inaction) affect the people who make success possible. When leaders take a step back and recognize these patterns, they have the power to rebuild trust and reconnect their teams, thus creating a workplace where people want to be fired up for their work, which is indeed possible.

Transparency involves openly discussing successes, failures, and lessons learned. It also entails engaging in difficult conversations when necessary to ensure alignment with the company's vision and goals. A transparent workplace culture cannot be achieved without sincere and open communication. Regular feedback is another essential aspect; employees require clarity on their performance relative to objectives, while managers benefit from constructive feedback on their effectiveness. Effective feedback shouldn't be limited to annual performance reviews but should instead be an ongoing process to enhance transparency and accountability. According to Gallup research, employees value feedback as it helps them prioritize tasks and boost engagement levels significantly. Statistics indicate that those who receive meaningful feedback weekly are four times more likely to be engaged. Establishing a transparent organizational culture requires deliberate effort and continual focus; it does not occur spontaneously but through consistent dedication and purpose. All of this impacts an employee's well-being, and your employee's well-being matters!

Let's explore how an employee's personal life can impact the workplace. Separating work and life can pose a considerable challenge. In the opening of this book, I recounted an experience from my HR career journey where I learned firsthand how personal circumstances can profoundly influence professional life. Life is replete with ups and downs, and inevitably, challenges arise. Whether grappling with health issues, relationship strains, or other obstacles, no one's life unfolds flawlessly. As working individuals, we cannot expect immunity from these issues, and they often reverberate in our professional performance. When contending with mental health challenges or stress, maintaining focus on tasks or even attendance at work can prove arduous. It's normal to feel overwhelmed, and it's acceptable if these sentiments impact our job performance. Many circumstances are beyond our control, and experiencing stress or despondency is a natural reaction to life's trials. Occasionally, these emotions inevitably spill over into our professional realm. Attending to familial needs may supersede work obligations during a personal tragedy or urgency. In less acute scenarios, managing everyday stressors from home may require strategies to mitigate their impact on work.

We cannot always influence external events, but we can acknowledge that experiencing stress or despondency is normal. These feelings may occasionally disrupt our work, and that's understandable. When significant issues arise, they may demand immediate attention. For routine stressors, adopting coping mechanisms can facilitate a better equilibrium between work and personal life. Consider that the average person spends eight hours at work, amounting to a third of their day. Consequently, when work hours extend beyond the standard eight hours, the time for managing personal affairs diminishes. In the bustling business landscape, a poignant narrative elucidates a company's response when its employees confront personal adversities. It's a tale of compassion, human connection, and the profound impact of kindness within organizational precincts.

Leaders are like the compass that helps their team members navigate life's twists and turns while showing by example what it means to care honestly. Their actions and words set the tone for how everyone else behaves in the workplace. When leaders show that they genuinely care about their people, it sends a clear message: employees matter for what they do and who they are. Whether lending a compassionate ear, understanding someone else's perspective, or making decisions openly and honestly, leaders are the driving force behind a workplace culture that feels like a supportive family.

But it's not just about words, it's about actions, too. By giving their team members more responsibility and involving them in decision-making, leaders build trust and make everyone feel like they're part of something bigger. And when people feel trusted and valued, they're more likely to go above and beyond to help the company succeed. Communication is the glue that holds it all together. Leaders should be open and transparent, sharing information freely and listening attentively to what their team has to say. Whether through regular team meetings, personal check-ins, or anonymous feedback channels, keeping the lines of communication open builds a sense of trust and belonging.

And let's not forget the power of a simple "thank you." Recognizing and appreciating employees for their hard work and dedication goes a long way in boosting morale and reinforcing a culture of appreciation. However, leaders must also remember that their employees have lives outside of work. Encouraging a healthy work-life balance by offering flexible schedules and supporting mental health initiatives shows leaders care about their team's well-being. When leaders prioritize their people, employees feel more engaged, motivated, and loyal. Ultimately, leadership is not just about hitting business targets; it's about creating a warm and welcoming environment where everyone feels valued, supported, and empowered to be their best selves.

Now let's talk about your life. Take a moment to think about your day-to-day life and all your current activities. For some, it's the mundane routine. For others, it's the children, the spouse, or a loved one. And for some of you, you think I'm single, it's just me. Yeah, you and those bills. Life be life-ing, and we all have to think about those outside stressors that are causing us anxiety. No one is immune. When the demands of life exceed your resources and coping abilities, your mental health can be impacted.

You take a moment to breathe.

Everything around us is shifting, new systems, new expectations, tighter deadlines, and it can begin to feel like the ground never stops moving. And when one truly stops to think about it, how does that make you feel? Then, imagine yourself as someone else in your workplace, perhaps another team member, someone managed by you, or someone who talks rarely. How might they feel in this season of change?

If you are a leader at all right now, especially in the middle or at the top, you probably are carrying more than people know. You look composed from the outside, strategic, responsive, maybe even unshakable. But inside? You may feel like you are holding the walls up, with both hands, as everything shifts around you.

You are not alone. There is a special kind of pressure that accompanies leading from the middle. Your job is to understand and operate top-level strategies, even as you answer to the concrete human needs of the people who work for you. You take care of complaints, you manage conflict, you translate moving targets, and all the time, you are required to work as if nothing were wrong. Every word is weighed. Every decision is scrutinized. And during the whole mess, you are to act with steadiness and clarity. It's exhausting.

What many fail to grasp is how lonely it can be at the top. You're the person others turn to, the one receiving their questions, pleas, and solutions. You are the sense-maker. The mediator. The coach. The shield. But who is there for you when you're not feeling yourself? When you're overwhelmed? And when you are in doubt about your own confidence? Leadership is romanticized, but behind the curtain, it's lonely.

You're dealing with deadlines, budgets, and goals, but you're also attempting to handle team morale, interpersonal dynamics, and communication hurdles. All while responding to emails, writing performance reviews, and the invisible, emotional labor that leadership involves. And that's just the job. You also have a life beyond it, families to take care of, aging parents to check on, relationships to tend to, health issues to worry about, money to fret over, maybe even some grief. Life doesn't work that way because you're a leader. You have bills to pay, kids to raise, hearts to heal. And yet, the presumption still is that you leave all that behind at the door and lead.

It is not fair, and it is not sustainable.

The truth is, we see you. Not perhaps the specifics of what it is you're holding, but the imprint of your leadership is in evidence, sometimes in small ways: an unruffled team in chaos, a change in culture, a tough conversation that took a turn. You are the reason a brother, mother, father, daughter, girlfriend, neighbor, or friend didn't give up. You're the one who got work done with heart. You are the reason your team still thinks it is worth trying. But in providing that for others, it's easy to lose track of yourself.

You turn into a function rather than a human being. A name in place of a human. You give and give, and if there's nothing in place to refill your tank, even the most resilient among us will start operating on fumes. And that's what we should discuss: your needs. Because you matter. Not just your results, not your decisions, though, but you. You deserve rest. You deserve care. You need mentorship, encouragement, and support that does not come with performance metrics. You should never have to earn being human; you are human already.

Leaders frequently say, "I don't have time to get help," or "I don't want to appear weak." But reaching out for help is not a weakness; it is wisdom. Whether it's coaching, a safe space to vent, wellness resources, peer support, or a quiet moment of reflection, there could be tools available for you. They aren't rewards. They're necessities. And it's all right if you're not all right.

The bar you may have been setting yourself in is inhuman, but you are not. You are allowed to be tired. You are entitled to question. You are allowed to pause. The work will wait. You can't pour from an empty cup.

If we only mention leadership development in a crisis, it is much too late. And if we invest only in frontline employees and forget the people they work for, we miss the point entirely. Because your well-being determines theirs. Your experience of this work is contagious, for better or worse. Let's do better for you. Let's create systems that support you as you support everyone else. Let's stop pretending resilience is synonymous with silence, and let's start to define strength as something that involves care, tenderness, and boundaries.

You are not just a role. You are more than an agent of productivity. You are a person. You are a leader. And you are seen. So, if the weight is too much today, feel free to put some of it down. Support exists. You don't have to earn it. You are already eligible: Just by carrying more than most. And the next time you think to yourself, "Is any of this worth it?" Remember this: yes, it does. And so do you.

And then there's the Family Medical Leave Act (FMLA). Even hearing the acronym is enough to make some people groan. For some, the first thought when they hear "FMLA" is, "Well, this is going to be complicated," or "I hope it's not getting abused."

But let's suspend that response for a moment.

What if, under all that paperwork, someone is quietly struggling? Someone navigating anxiety, their health issue, caring for a loved one, or simply trying to withstand the constant swirl of change. Have we ever stopped to inquire what's behind these spikes in FMLA requests? Change fatigue is real, and not always accompanied by tears or tantrums. Sometimes it's quiet apathy. Quiet absenteeism. Missed deadlines. And yes, sometimes it's FMLA.

In this situation, both employers and employees can do so individually and collectively. Talk to yourself. It's okay not to be OK. Requiring support is not weak; it's human. Know your rights and where to turn when you need help. FMLA is there to protect you during tough times. Don't wait for things to reach breaking point before you ask for help. Let someone you trust know if you're having trouble. You don't have to share all the details, but earlier support can prevent a crisis later.

If you're the manager:

Empathy in decision making. Instead of automatically suspecting abuse, ask yourself, "What could be happening here?" Remember that each of your employees is different, and you can't manage them all the same.

Make clear to your team that it's okay to seek help. Sometimes just hearing "You're not alone" makes all the difference. Signs to watch for. Is a person uncommunicative? Is he or she missing more days than usual, or showing up but not present? These are the occasions when you express concern, not judgment. Treat "Guilt-free" as an example. Leading in this way gives others the space to do likewise. It's not always about performance. Sometimes it's about understanding what is really behind the performance issues. And if you can't keep up with everything either, that's all right. You are not failing; you're adapting in an environment where tomorrow always seems to ask far more of us than yesterday did. One question our society needs to pose a lot more frequently is: How are we doing as a whole?

Let's make our workplace settings that don't make FMLA requests a cause for alarm, but rather an alarm: telling us that we need room to care for ourselves and each other. That every request has a person behind it. And sometimes, what those people most need is to be seen.

Now that we have discussed the importance of seeing employees as people, let's talk about why HR can expand its role beyond enforcing policies. HR professionals can expand their role beyond enforcing policies by actively engaging with employee well-being. This includes wellness programs, mental health support, and career development opportunities. For example, HR can organize workshops on stress management, provide access to counseling services, and create mentorship programs. By focusing on these areas, HR helps foster a supportive and growth-oriented environment. This broader role positively impacts employee morale, increasing job satisfaction and productivity. Additionally, it contributes to a healthier organizational culture where employees feel valued and supported, ultimately benefiting the company's overall success.

HR professionals are often in the delicate position of enforcing company policy while managing staff members with unique needs. Applying policies rigidly can guarantee even-handedness and uniformity, but at times, it may not be in the best interest of each employee or the organization. Flexible Policy Application: Translates into a supportive and adaptable culture.

For example, take a company that only permits remote work one day per week. However, an employee who suffers from a chronic illness asked for extended work-from-home days to ensure better management of the condition. Something as simple as an accommodation policy to allow HR to make this exception, permitting the employee to work from home three days a week, would result in a happier employee who is more productive and loyal to the company. The organization could keep a team member who served them exceedingly well and demonstrated their commitment to supporting an inclusive work culture, as they were agile enough to adapt to this policy.

Human emotions are at the heart of workplace interactions and decision-making. Positive emotions, like enthusiasm, can inspire teamwork and creativity, while negative emotions, such as frustration, can lead to conflicts and hinder cooperation. Emotions also play a significant role in motivation and performance; feeling good boosts productivity and engagement, while feeling stressed or burnt out can lead to absenteeism and inefficiency. Awareness of emotion helps make balanced decisions, which is crucial for a healthy work environment.

Employees often face emotional challenges that can be easily overlooked. Stress and anxiety are everyday issues, driven by high workloads, tight deadlines, and job insecurity. These pressures can take a toll on well-being and productivity. Prolonged stress can lead to burnout, leaving employees emotionally drained and less effective in their roles. Additionally, a lack of social connections can lead to feelings of isolation, affecting mental health and job engagement. It's important to note that this issue is not solely attributable to remote work. Companies sometimes attribute isolation to remote work, but it's crucial to recognize six generations in the workplace (yes, six), each with different preferences and needs.

One common misconception is that bringing employees into the office will foster bonding. However, if unclear strategies and directions mark office interactions, engagement may not improve. The pandemic has fundamentally shifted perspectives on work, and it's essential to avoid imposing personal biases, such as a preference for in-office work, on others. The younger generation is adept at identifying insincerity, which can lead to increased resentment and distrust. Interpersonal conflicts and dissatisfaction with job roles can cause frustration and resentment. Employees who feel undervalued or unrecognized may become demotivated and disengaged. These emotional challenges can be easily missed by HR, leading to a decline in workplace morale and productivity. HR must recognize and address these issues to maintain a positive work environment.

Hold on, let's sit right here for a minute. Lacking accountability is not just a tiny leadership flaw; it's one of the reasons people feel bitter, disengaged from work, and at odds with each other. When there's no accountability, trust ebbs away, tempers flare, and staff start to feel their efforts are all for naught.

So, what does real accountability look like? It starts at the top. Leaders set the course not by demanding accountability from those below them but by showing it themselves. That means owning up to mistakes, confessing when communication isn't clear, and recognizing when things could have been handled more appropriately. It's not about being perfect; it's about being truthful.

When you're in charge, it's easy to think you're being clear and transparent, especially when trying to balance priorities, make hard decisions, and spare your team from unnecessary stress. However, when a leader comes off as not being transparent, even inadvertently, it can create absolute havoc in the organization. Some people will feel left out or confused. They may question decisions or

Would you be contributing to the problem? Here are some red flags to watch for:

- Your team isn't raising their voices as often, or they appear reluctant to give feedback.
- You're discovering problems from others, rather than hearing them directly.
- There's a sense that people are checked out or feel flat on the team.
- There is quiet resistance, stalling, failure to follow up, or missed deadlines.
- The same issues keep surfacing, even after you thought they were fixed.
- People are eager to agree but not to act or propose new ideas.
- People start distancing themselves from you or only come to you as a last resort.

The most important thing: watch out for the "inner circle" trap. Even with the best intentions, it's easy to slip into a pattern of relying on a few go-to people. Perhaps you think alike or have developed loyalty and trust over the years. But when do outsiders begin to feel like outsiders looking in? It can cause real damage. It creates a divide. People stop raising their hands, stop sharing ideas, and stop even trying because they feel like decisions are already being made without them. An "inner circle" dynamic erodes trust and morale, whether real or perceived. It sends the unwitting message that entry and equity are a function of proximity, not merit or promise. So, what can you do to fix it? Here's where you can start:

- wonder what's going on behind closed doors. Such uncertainty can erode morale, impede collaboration, and, over time, result in disengagement, if not turnover. On the other hand, when leaders are transparent, offering what they know, and most importantly, what they don't know, and explaining the "why" behind their decisions, it fosters trust, clarity, and connection. Ask for feedback genuinely. Give your team room to tell you what's working and what's not working. Be open, not defensive. Even simply asking lets them know that you care.
- Recognize your own mistakes. You don't need to be perfect, only real. Telling the truth when you've come short establishes trust more quickly than pretending you didn't.
- Share what you know and what you don't. You don't have to have all the answers. They need to believe you're being truthful to them.
- Explain the "why." Even when the decision is complex or controversial, individuals respect the ability to understand the rationale behind it.
- Show up. Be present. Don't underestimate the value of a quick check-in, an open-door moment, or simply asking, "How are you holding up?"

- Ensure that everyone has a seat at the table. Rotate opportunities, request ideas in different ways (written, spoken, small groups), and listen when people speak up.
- Follow through. Do what you say you'll do. And when you can't, circle back and say why.
- Break the bubble. Look at who you instinctively turn to and extend yourself beyond that circle. You may be amazed at the value of others when they feel they are seen and included.

You don't need to change everything at once. Beginning with one small step, one honest conversation, one moment of inclusion, one act of vulnerability. Transparency is not a once-off announcement; it's a practice. And when people see you doing it, they'll do as you do. It can also be an example of how to fix this.

Leadership Note Example:

Hey team, I wanted to talk about something pervasive in almost every work environment, sometimes silent but always compelling, and that is how we show up as leaders, in terms of transparency. We may not always appreciate this, but when people feel they're not receiving the complete story, it opens room for confusion, speculation, and mistrust. And the hard part? Sometimes we're doing our best to shield the team from extra turbulence, holding back until we have thorough answers, but there still seems to be something wrong in the eyes of others. So, how can you tell if there might be a disconnect?

Here are some signs that might be worth heeding:

- People are participating less in meetings, and the same voices dominate all the time.
- You hear about team concerns secondhand or late.
- The vibe has changed; there is more silence, hesitation, or distance.
- Some appear in "the loop," while others appear shocked or checked out.
- Turnover or burnout is slowly creeping up.

When one feels disconnected from us, there's a challenging but fundamental part: we don't always realize we are a part of the problem. And it doesn't mean we are bad leaders. It means we're human. One of the greatest (and least understood; also: harmful) habits that can seed itself is what I refer to as the "inner circle" mentality, that is, we start to lean on the same few people to inform decisions, or lead conversations, or provide input. It seems efficient, perhaps even comforting. But to the rest of the team? It can feel like doors are shut and trust is contingent. People stop participating wholeheartedly when they don't feel part of the whole. They check out. They play it safe. And what extraordinary insight, creativity, and heart do they contribute? It stays tucked away. So, what can we do? Hierarchical structures perpetuate exclusion and misunderstandings about different environments to date.

Stop and welcome new voices. Don't just rely on your "go-tos." Survey a quieter person for their thoughts. Bring in someone who hasn't been in the process before. Talk even when you're not confirmed. A brief "Here's what I know, here's what we're doing, and here's what I'll let you know next" can go far. Be honest, not perfect. People connect with reality. You're not expected to have everything figured out; just let them in. Notice your patterns. Who are you constantly copying? Who are you unintentionally excluding?

Make time for connection. Not status checks but real check-ins. When in doubt, ask: "What do you need from me right now?" This can shift everything. And lastly, if you suspect some rebuilding may be required, keep it small. One conversation. One moment of vulnerability. An invitation to one out there who's been sitting on the sidelines. Leadership doesn't mean you're perfect; it means you're aware, you're open, and you're willing to grow.

Employees take notes when a leader steps up to the plate. It creates psychological safety, allowing teams to do likewise without fear of blame or reprisal. It generates respect because people are much more willing to walk behind a leader who practices what he preaches. And above all, it creates an environment where growth, learning, and trust can flourish. On the other hand, if leaders shift responsibility, make excuses, or raise standards for others that they don't meet, the result is ill will. People begin to tune out and chat in hallways, and eventually, they pull out, sometimes emotionally, sometimes literally. Leadership is not about being right every time. It is also about truthfulness, responsibility, and creating an environment where everyone participates.

First, leadership has to stand up and be counted. Second, let us not forget that power reflects the quality of management behind any organization. A leader cannot become indifferent. Take, for example, the following harmful behavior:

- Defensiveness. As humans, we tend to shrug off truths that pinch a nerve. If an employee has a critical discussion in the presence of his group members, straying from the conversation off track turns it into a one-on-one discussion. Take that frequent habit as an example, and if this talk wanders off too far, we are not here today for a wrap-up on what our man did wrong last year, but about the employee now and how you can help make him or her better than they were. Again, I'd like to stress your sincere concern for the welfare of your subordinates, mentioning that you are strong for these people's futures with your organization.
- Passive Aggression: That is, you confront passive-aggressive communication head-on. "I hear you are unhappy about (policy, schedule, standard of behavior, etc.). This is what I learned from team members when they reported to me. If you have not spoken directly or told me about these fears, please discuss them with me."
- Bullying: When there is clear evidence that someone is being bullied, take adequate measures immediately. Have the hard stuff on what you've done or not done written down - consequences from those actions, if there's been any change, and when we can expect to check again.

You must know strongly enough to recognize when something isn't going your way. Every manager has at least one of these, a problematic employee to take care of, but try as you might, things are going less than peachy still anyhow... You've given Frank feedback and invested in his/her development. Have they all had support for all their needs? And set some standards? You've asked your people what they think or tried to find out what that means. But while we try our hardest, she or he does not want to improve. Putting someone in the disciplinary process, firing them before they resign, or hiring for a new position are not decisions that make a person feel good about themselves. However, one should do these things only if they are sure the employee has had every chance to succeed.

Indeed, just as in all other areas of life, human resource management also demands tools and methodologies to map the complex emotional landscape of an organization.

- Pulse surveys and feedback systems where responses are kept anonymous provide a broad-brush picture: overall, things seem satisfactory, or everyone feels above average levels emotionally.
- Feedback focus groups and one-on-one meetings, for example, are reasonable steps in this direction to try to take the temperature of your company.
- Additionally, you might look at people's HR statistics to discern trends: turnover the year after you came in third against previous years. Or suppose we find that although work absences have risen considerably from what they used to be before, then, in fact, output this time is better than ever - where are we going wrong?

Human resources can incorporate EQ (emotional quotient) into training programs and feedback mechanisms.

This will not only help leaders manage and control their feelings but also bring home the point that each member of an organization should be working for others' benefit as well as their own.

- Providing wellness programs and stress management workshops helps support emotional health and resilience. Examples of this assistance range from classes for meditative breathing to periods during which employees may quietly reflect on getting hold of themselves. Use Employee Assistance Programs (EAPs) to counsel employees on personal and work problems. Apply conflict resolution/mediation strategies to uncover hidden emotional climate variables so that we can manage them.
- Psychological-based organizational emotions theories and models are beneficial for people. Recognition and Management of Emotional Intelligence Theory from Daniel Goleman teaches you how to recognize and control your emotions; at the same time, Maslow's Hierarchy of Needs shows us that workers have different needs driven by their operating levels. It separates job satisfaction from job dissatisfaction.
- More models available for dealing with workplace emotions are the Job Demands-Resources (JD-R) Model and Social Exchange Theory. The JD-R Model posits that job demands and resources can lead to burnout unless a healthy balance is struck between them. On the other hand, social exchange theory suggests that employees should manage their relationships so

that they not only give but also reciprocate favors.

- Positive Psychology, focusing on the factors enabling people to live happy lives and experience well-being even under high pressure in society, also creates a good emotional climate.
- Whatever happens in their personal life will affect employee performance and behavior. For example, external factors such as financial problems, relationship difficulties, and health issues can directly affect your work. That translates either into sloppy performance or gets those under matters of an internal nature doing little more than fighting against physical difficulty. Anxiety diverts focus. It distracts us from our tasks and wastes our time.
- It also restricts our production ability, resulting in general discontent in our working environment. Not to mention that criticism runs rampant throughout the team since no one can feel good about themselves when they're not being recognized or challenged. Before you conclude that employees are lazy and in need of an undeserved raise, consider the following humane approaches:
- Reflect on Past Experience: Avoid automatically equating current wage and educational expectations with your history of earning and learning. It should be noted that economic conditions and employment market dynamics change over time.
- Admit the Current Cost of Living: Understand the present living environment so you know how difficult it has become financially for workers

today. Awareness breeds compassion: justice cannot be without fairness in wages and benefits.

- Critique Organizational Philosophy in Compensation: How does your company's compensation strategy compare with industry standards? Is it fair to employees to reward their input and output? Transparency creates trust and drives mutual effort.

- Stand Up for Deserving Workers: Identify and assist employees who set a performance standard. Paving their way forward through recognition and opportunity, on the other hand, encourages merit-based excellence.

- It's Time to Train Rising Stars: Devote resources to nurturing potential employees. Support their growth through mentoring, training, and other measures they need to evolve. The machine and its pieces all benefit.

Recognizing that some organizations may be financially limited, it is critical to understand how personal biases might affect your effectiveness in helping employees progress. Even though it's challenging to treat employees as independent-minded individuals who have their futures, there's no doubt that leaders should bring people up to a high level of striving, possibly surpassing any they may envision. By making your leadership empathetic and supportive, you create an environment where employees are valued and want to work hard. In so doing, it strengthens individual satisfaction and ensures general corporate success.

In some cases, personal affairs at home carry over into how they interact with people at work and their relationships with co-workers. An employee who struggles to get through a day can be less productive, which increases the pressure on subordinates to complete tasks by deadlines. A positive result of a supportive work environment usually solves long-term, chronic stress-induced problems on the job. This includes flexible attributes in work and personal life, such as counseling means and promoting employee well-being. Indeed, if you care about people's personal lives just as much as you do those lives devoted to your company, both must be healthy, then it is only logical that all sides will benefit from overall good health.

Human Resources is responsible for aiding the employees when personal affairs impinge on service. A hallmark HR role cultivates a company environment where the two tides of ultimate capital accumulation and sensitivity toward one's employees can coalesce. First, clear regulations must be established that respect everyone's limitations and give way to genuine respect for every worker's dignity. Such rules might include, for instance, introducing proper leave guidelines so employees can deal with personal problems without fear of encountering adverse psychological stress. This type of normative regulation makes for a good working environment, just like dirt-proof carpets; therefore, HR is responsible for ensuring that such norms are established on paper and followed up collectively by all workers in practice. HR is also improving the transparency and openness of communication within businesses. For instance, training managers and supervisors to counter stress or personal problems emerging from their employees is a good example. HR helps by educating leaders not to judge but to handle these situations tactfully. Subsequent meetings between staff and managers also serve this function well over time, for at that time, any issues that have arisen can be contained early, and workers may air their grievances out of sight behind those closed doors.

Another critical area is the provision of Employee Assistance Programs (EAPs). EAPs provide confidential counseling services and support for employees who have personal problems that may later hurt their job performance. HR should advocate for these services, letting employees know how to get involved. People can benefit significantly from having information about mental health resources, financial planning, and other like-minded services. However, human resources (HR) support also needs to be adaptable. For example, introducing flexible work policies such as telecommuting and flextime can help workers juggle personal and professional responsibilities simultaneously. These choices are nothing to belittle in people's eyes. How important they are can be seen in that this keeps employees in good, productive shape and shows a company that understands the needs of its staff and cares for them.

HR must also ensure that support does not degenerate into discrimination and favoritism. Every instance must be dealt with equitably and in the strictest confidence possible; Support must be administered fairly and consistently. Similarly, specific instructions on handling personal matters can prevent certain people from being biased or given unequal treatment. The goal of this training and development program introduced by the HR Office is to promote orientation towards life, not just work, not just accomplishing things promptly, but doing them well. With these programs, employees learn methods for coping, becoming established in a new company, and reducing the effect of their private life on their work. In summary, you establish a culture of empathy and understanding. Regularly inform your employees that the more prominent culture in which they live gives them an atmosphere where they should be able to take time off without being judged. Acknowledging victories and accomplishments, boosting morale among good workers, and understanding the hardships of employees would create a better environment for all. This is also one way HR can see to it that people can carry off both their challenges and their professional responsibilities at the same time.

CHAPTER 3
Case Studies: Tales of Woe, Misfortune, and Toxic Leadership

Case Study: Let's visit Company X, once a much-lauded model of innovation and a beacon of the vibrant workplace. But as it grew, cracks began to appear. Employees felt stretched thin, unappreciated, and distant from upper management. Even with the echo of their complaints, the change they sought never materialized, and morale sank. Company X's culture, HR, Jackson lamented, "it was as if we were in a hamster wheel of death and couldn't get off, and we felt unseen". Disaster hit when Sarah (a shining light that burned itself out tragically) lost the battle she fought within herself. An investigation exposed toxic undercurrents in the culture of the workplace, adding to Sarah's struggles with depression.

Analysis: Company X's toxic culture resulted from a number of causes:

- **Unmanageable workloads:** Officers were overwhelmed by unmanageable caseloads, causing stress and burnout.
- **Communication breakdown:** A gulf opened between the grunts on the ground and the suits making decisions, leading to frustration and resentment.
- **Lack of support:** There were limited mental health resources, leaving workers to grapple with their struggles on their own.
- **Culture of fear:** Concern of retaliation silenced speakers, preventing the airing of grievances.

- **Consequences:** The fallout from Company X's poison had terrible effects.
- **Brain drains:** Good workers were being driven away by burnout and frustration, and expertise was being lost.
- **Reputation decline:** Sarah's demise reflected badly on Company X; it hurt hiring and client relations.
- **Legal complications:** The company risked lawsuits for failing to create a safe work environment.
- **Lessons Learned:** The story of Company X is a reminder of how crucial it is to focus on people when structuring organizations.
- **HR endeavors should focus on:** Balancing life and work and having a flexible schedule and a manageable workload to prevent burning out.
- **Promoting Transparent Dialogue**: To create a culture that encourages open communication in which all voices are recognized and heard, regardless of hierarchy.
- **Mental wellness advocacy:** Making resources available to help support systems be put in place and breaking down the stigma around mental health discussion.
- **Accountability:** Leadership is held responsible for creating environments of empathy and for meaningfully addressing any issues brought forward.

Through incorporating the key learnings from Company X's journey, businesses can aim to create work environments that breed success and rest assured that their employees are taken care of first and foremost. Bad management creates a toxic work environment. Destructive phenomena such as toxic leadership go against the psychological and physical health of the organization and the individual. It is a syndrome of behaviors in which leaders place their own agendas above the well-being of their team and the welfare of their organization. This poisonous behavior seeps throughout the company, affecting every level of staff. While bad leaders can be good at their jobs, they inspire and spread negativity in the workplace by way of their impact, not to a certain number of people.

According to recent research released by Life Meets Work Consulting, 56% of workers are handed the wrong kind of leader, and that leads to a bad work environment. What's surprising is that around one-third of leaders are prone to it. Leadership toxicity might have many sources, such as when leaders pursue their own interests at the expense of the long-term welfare of the organization. This destructive leadership style may result in decreased productivity through increased employee absenteeism and sick leave, and consequently decreased employee performance, which is caused by reduced commitment and job dissatisfaction. To make things worse for companies, it is about handling the negative impacts of toxic leaders when they don't have the right experience or resources to intervene. These people suffer more than most, because they pick up the social tab for the dysfunction of these leaders. The problem is that too few leaders understand that they're toxic, and what's even worse is that there are company executives who understand these characteristics yet are reluctant to rock the boat to deal with them.

As HR professionals, it is up to us to make a compelling argument to upper management about why we should address instead of ignoring the risks or turn a blind eye to this behavior. The hidden costs of which can represent a serious threat to the well-being of the organization. Recently, the industry has been shining a light on the darker side of leadership, as studies delve into the harm that toxic leadership has on mental health in the workplace and ultimately on businesses. One must understand that toxic leadership is not only ineffective, but also the way one leads.

Toxic leadership is a shadow that sneaks in when it is least expected in the leadership landscape; it spreads silently, usually so silently that it is almost indistinguishable, like a subtle venom. And its influence does not stop at individuals but runs through teams and can also affect the entire organization. The research finds that toxic leadership is the source of many problems. It makes people want to quit their jobs, feel miserable at work, and even have problems like anxiety and burnout. It's hard because while experts insist that toxic behavior damages how effectively the organization learns and performs, the leaders who behave that way don't always recognize it as a problem. They believe what they're doing is fine. A fascinating phenomenon, not always so, as it explains why toxic leaders continue to behave the way that they do. A company that dismisses such problems may underestimate the extent to which it's implicitly approving of toxicity, of bad behavior. If you perceive an office culture where some individuals are more favored than others, a toxic leader may be to blame. Leaders can even, at times, inadvertently form cliques and build barriers, leaving some of the workforce on the outside. This may occur when leaders focus more on personal connections than qualifications, resulting in an "in-group" and an "out-group." Pitting employees against each other by promoting, rewarding, and helping only those who are in your inner circle or are considered go-to or loyal confidants does nothing more than foster a culture of haves and have-nots.

Here are 10 reasons we should be against such exclusivity, and yes, that includes people who are members of the "in group." It may even cause stress, anxiety, mental health problems, or the feeling of being bullied in the workplace. Micromanagers are also toxic leaders; they will attempt to control everything and anything they can, which can lead to burnout and stress on their team. If you find they micromanage, the leader may have trust or control issues. Opening a conversation about why it becomes difficult for them to trust their team can go a long way toward resolving the underlying issue. The fact is, almost every organization will have to contend with toxic leaders at some point. We all need to be held accountable and to learn, grow, and be better for having done so. It's going to take the help of at least one other person to solve this behavior, because the leader who is infected by the behavior is not able to know how he shows up to his team or to the people in the organization. How do you know if YOU are the leader? Toxic leaders share the following characteristics: self-serving, manipulative, and destructive to an organization.

Lack of Honesty and Consistency

Behavior: Frequently changes expectations or backtracks on decisions without clear communication. This dishonesty creates confusion and erodes trust.

Solution: Commit to transparency and consistency. If decisions must change, explain the reason clearly. Keep written records of key expectations to avoid misalignment. Practice accountability: and own up to mistakes and correct them publicly when needed.

Ignores Feedback

Behavior: Dismisses team input and insists on being right, blocking opportunities for growth and innovation.

Solution: Ask for feedback regularly (in meetings, anonymous surveys, etc.). Act on what you hear to show you're listening. Build psychological safety by responding to criticism with openness, not defensiveness.

Arrogance and Close-mindedness

Behavior: Believes they are always right, resists being questioned, and expects blind agreement.

Solution: Practice humility. Acknowledge when you're wrong and show appreciation for diverse perspectives. Encourage healthy debate. Ask, "What am I missing?" to invite alternative views.
Model vulnerability as a strength, not a weakness.

Overemphasis on Hierarchy
Behavior: Relies on formal authority and rank to assert control, discouraging collaboration and flattening creativity.

Solution: Empower others to lead based on expertise, not title. Use positional power to elevate others, not dominate them. Foster a culture of mutual respect over rigid roles.

Discriminatory or Biased Behavior
Behavior: Shows favoritism or biases based on race, gender, age, orientation, or personal relationships. Personal relationships are a big one; this can often be seen as your go-to person. And most leaders don't see this as biased behavior.

Solution: Commit to inclusive leadership. Educate yourself on unconscious bias and inclusive practices. Apply rules and rewards equitably. Create a safe space for team members to raise DEI (Diversity, Equity, Inclusion) concerns.

Lack of Confidence
Behavior: Insecurity leads to micromanaging or defensiveness. Distrust of team members is common.

Solution: Build self-awareness through coaching or reflection. Delegate meaningfully and trust others to deliver. Focus on continuous learning rather than perfection.

Incompetence or Poor Decision-Making
Behavior: Struggles to fulfill responsibilities, makes poor decisions, and shifts blame to others.

Solution: Identify skill gaps and invest in professional development. Surround yourself with people who have strengths you lack and let them lead. Take responsibility for mistakes and treat them as learning opportunities.

Self-Serving Leadership
Behavior: Prioritizes personal ambition over team success and uses leadership as a stepping stone rather than a responsibility.

Solution: Align your success with team success. Celebrating collective wins publicly. Mentor and develop others, be known for building leaders, not just rising fast. Conduct regular "pulse checks" with your team to ensure they feel valued and supported.

Seeing these qualities in yourself, if you do, is the first, and often the most powerful step toward change. Organizations can use Various Approaches to address and prevent toxic leadership.

Firstly, in terms of leader recruitment and succession, focus on the screening and selection methods. Promoting or hiring people for a leadership position is critical in any business because it has a massive impact on team productivity and, in turn, on the company's success. But the cost of moving or hiring someone who isn't right can also be damaging. The organization has a responsibility to find and grow its best talent. Sadly, far too many companies continue to promote people into management who have never been taught a lick about what I'd like to call basic skills for the basic man, or woman, for that matter. On the other hand, hiring for **loyalty** and not for alignment of talent with what the company needs has its downside as well.

Whether you believe it's fair or not is another question, but the reality is these kinds of mistakes can have big implications, including the loss of talented employees. One bad hire or promotion can set off a chain reaction throughout an entire team. Your best people will feel unappreciated and unwanted, and feelings of resentment that may lead them to lash out in a job search. The departure of these individuals may have a serious effect on the organization's performance and morale and ultimately, negatively impact the bottom line. On the contrary, moving the right people up can change the whole company for the better. It can raise spirits, boost productivity, and create a more supportive working environment. When workers believe that their efforts, loyalty, and commitment are recognized and appreciated, they will stay more committed and more engaged, contributing to the success of the overall organization.

When you have chosen the correct leadership, the next stage is to continue to grow them. Organizations can't afford to drag their feet when it comes to investing in leadership development. Most organizations have more pressing priorities and believe (incorrectly, as they won't get to those results if they wait to invest in leadership training) that they can put off leadership development to focus on results that will come faster.

They tend to be of the "we will solve it, when stabilized" kind, or they start programs after a lot of program planning. It's not a postponement but only a delay anyway, and it only benefits them. Consider where you want to be in a year. Do you want to be a raw novice in the cultivation of your leadership capabilities, or would you prefer to be up and running in Generation Two? You're investing in leadership development now and laying the foundation for success. When you put resources into leadership development, you're investing in more than just your leaders; you're investing in the capacity of your team and the future of your company. So why wait? Begin by blazing the path to a brighter future. If you don't invest in the leadership that knows where you are today and where you are going, you could go out of business.

We often think of such brands as Sears, Blockbuster, and Radio Shack, the great old-timers of yesteryear. The good news is that such companies didn't have any effective leadership development programs in place, and their negligence led to fatal consequences in many important areas. Consider the case of Sears. They used to be the source of everything, right? But they went off course somehow. They stopped investing in their people, stopped listening to what customers wanted." And you know what happened next. Or how about Circuit City? Remember them? They were big, but they were also capable of making some pretty big mistakes. Such as when they laid off a lot of experienced staff to save money. Yes, it saved them money in the short term, but it led to a drain in the long term. People were not returning because they no longer received the quality of service. And there is also Blockbuster and

Radio Shack. They did not embrace new technology and were not flexible with the times. They could have been Netflix or Amazon, but they didn't. Yes, it's tempting to gaze upon these companies and say, "Well, they just couldn't keep up" or "You should have just done things the way you've always done them. But let's be honest, it was about more than that. It was about leadership, about keeping your people safe, about being prepared to change when that need arose. Because otherwise, well, then you know that you can end up on the wrong side of history.

There are a few dynamics occurring in today's workplace for organizations to be aware of. There are certainly benefits to sticking with a company for years and moving up the ranks through internal promotions. But it also comes with its fair share of issues. Starvation, a measure of loyalty and patience for so many years, may no longer be effective as companies increasingly value innovation over longevity. A major reason is that each generation has different values and expectations, which define their experiences. So, how did we get here: To a place where Boomer and Gen X employees have seen their parents stick around somewhere for years and then retire without much fuss, without much reward? They described that experience as formative for them in the way they perceive loyalty and stability in a job. People are frequently undervalued as workers, and a sense of loyalty is valued, but not sacrifices over the years, committed to a lifetime.

Is it really a surprise, then, that the younger generations have noticed? On the other hand,

Millennials and Gen Z are coming up into an economy where technology is moving fast, and what careers will exist years from now can literally change overnight. Long-term loyalty doesn't necessarily result in job security or career advancement, they point out. This has put Millennials and now Gen Z staff in the same boat, now with culture, business & coaching prompts to get on with in a motivated culture, you can read more about.

Many say they are likely to remain for only four or five years before they look for new opportunities. They leave sooner because they can build a career and live by deadlines all the time; not that he or she is not serious or committed, but what if I want to pursue something else? Organizations that do not adapt to these new expectations may have trouble with the retention and engagement of employees. This resistance to change can be observed in the fact that these long-term workers might not be as willing to embrace change, and their perceived hostility can hinder the progress of the organization. Sometimes it is fear that is doing the resisting. Fear of being weak or not seen as the "subject matter expert." Secondary truth: Some of these people may have worked too hard and too long to back into this "title", to then turn around and accept that someone with a "new" idea walked in and, with technology, made the process that

I put in place years ago seem antiquated. It's also about power. You'll find this a lot in complex-looking organizations. It's not a complex organization. The real problem is that the knowledge-bearers aren't sharing the knowledge. Ie, the processes are very much not transparent. It means you need to deal with the power broker to get what you want.

Businesses must address this by investing in robust Learning and Development (L&D) programs that incorporate ongoing training as an essential part of the company culture. This way, employees are always upskilled in order to keep pace with a more agile work environment. Those employers who perceive Millennials and Gen Z as lazy or who imagine that they are entitled to ask for a higher salary straight out of college do so at their peril. These are generations of the most technically talented, innovative workforce we have ever seen. Everybody feels at a slight remove and is out looking for an organization that will respect their skills and allow them to learn. But they don't do as well with outdated practices or the 'you work for me' culture.

Remember, it is a worker's market, not the other way around, which was brought on by the pandemic. But many companies are still clinging to traditional management strategies that simply don't fit our younger and younger workforce. The old methods of some physical exercise, team exercises, and the whole "parachute in, parachute out" philosophy get old and can often backfire by creating a gap, where younger team members feel that they are just not contributing, or worse, things are slowing their growth. In response, Millennials and Gen Zers are presently seeking to be valued more in the workplace, seeking more flexibility, respect, and opportunity. Businesses must be aware of these generational differences and adapt to remain competitive and to retain and attract good employees.

One of the ways to close those generational gaps is to foster innovation and provide opportunities for career advancement and professional development. It would also plant a culture where every single employee will believe he is valued and that they have to bring their A game. Plus, the more open communication you have between generations, the more peace will reign in your workplace (and life). The ability to see the strengths and different things each generation brings to an organization means that a group of people in the company or anywhere else can all work together as one team. And this, in turn, not only makes employees feel good, but it also makes businesses more successful.

Ultimately, the upshot may be that any business that cannot grow with a burgeoning workforce not only runs the risk of losing its best employees but can also be left behind in a fast-moving market. Meeting the needs of, and the expectations from, each generation of organizations results in agile, adaptable teams that are well prepared for modern business challenges. In summary, understanding workforce trends and engaging all generations is essential to the advancement of an organization. That requires ongoing innovation and creation, and creating an environment that also works for all ages, to build a foundation that is sustainable for long-term engagement.

And what kind of leader is preferable to manage a heterogeneous group of employees with a wide array of needs and expectations? It lies in leadership that is anchored with strong emotional intelligence and a balanced sense of empathy. It is leaders like these that we need in our workplaces, leaders who can get to the bottom of the complex work environment we have today and make sure everyone feels respected and inspired. The leader with high EI is important because they can recognize and regulate their own emotions and those of others. They're able to adapt to the very pulse and beat of the worker, and respond to their needs and concerns with a sense of understanding and perceptiveness.

Leaders with high emotional intelligence are able to establish strong relationships and trust, and the result of this is that employees feel heard and understood in the workplace. Empathy is essential for successful leadership in the increasingly diverse workspace of today. Empathetic leaders are those who lead with empathy and can step into the shoes of their employees and see and acknowledge their point of view and struggles.

It's this empathetic perspective that allows them to be able to come from a place where everyone's story is unique, everyone is struggling in different ways, and everyone has different feelings and emotions. At the same time, it is crucial for the leaders to enforce discipline with a firm but fair hand. Being tough is about establishing standards, holding people to them, and making tough choices when needed. Of course, this steadfastness should be tempered with fairness; that is, all employees should be treated with fairness, and decisions should be made on the basis of merit and openness. A leader who is high in emotional intelligence and empathy, while also fair, fosters a work environment in which employees feel honored and respected.

These leaders are skilled at maneuvering through complex interpersonal relationships, handling conflicts skillfully, and being able to drive their teams to be their most successful. This balanced approach leads to higher levels of employee engagement and morale.

Furthermore, leaders who have these traits are better prepared for the challenges of leading a multi-generational workforce. They know how different generations think and what their expectations and standards are, and are able to treat them in an empathic and inclusive way. It serves to build a sense of one team with everyone as an equal contributor. A leader with strong emotional intelligence can also handle stress and pressure well, which makes them a good role model for the team. These types of leaders contribute to keeping the working climate stable and offer support by showing resilience and a calm attitude, even in difficult situations. This builds and enhances general organizational stability and personal employee readiness of its workforce.

Professional growth and development leaders are more likely to identify and support the unique gifts and abilities of their workers, enabling them to grow both in their careers and their talents. This support fosters a sense of ownership in their work and the company. So basically, the right leader for today's diverse workforce is one with high emotional intelligence and leads with empathy, but with a strong hand, too. These leaders can develop supportive relationships, a supportive work environment, and fulfill the diverse employee expectations and needs. Their moderated perspective then adds to the competitive performance both as members of the team and as the team, which largely explains the success and survival of the organization.

CHAPTER 4

Reading the Room: Tools and Strategies for Understanding and Managing the Emotional Landscape of an Organization

The morale and attitude in any organization are a subtle and dynamic force. You can't put it on a balance sheet, but you can feel it in a meeting room, hear it in the silence of an overburdened team, or see it on the faces of a successful group. But reading and dealing with these emotional undercurrents is not a luxury of life for HR professionals; it's a necessity.

Feelings are slippery targets, but ones that affect morale, motivation, productivity, teamwork, and the desire of workers to stick around. Knowing a company's emotional pulse can be the difference between a thriving culture and a toxic one. HR professionals can start gaining an understanding of this emotional landscape by listening and observing actively. Leaders and HR professionals are frequently buried in data, reports, and deadlines, failing to notice the unexpressed needs of the people they work with. Something as basic as a virtual "How are you doing today?" or bridge-the-gaps coffee chat may uncover far more truths than a formal survey. Establishing a few safe zones that are free of retribution or chastisement, and where people can simply say what is on their mind, is essential in unveiling what the real motivators and sabotages are for a team.

One of the greatest influencers of how we manage our emotions at work is psychological safety, which was coined by Harvard professor Amy Edmondson. If we have a situation in which employees are free to voice their ideas and concerns without fear of humiliation or retribution, they are more likely to speak up, work together, and innovate. HR can help create an environment in which it encourages open communication and acknowledges workers' contributions, and instills in their products that feedback is not only accepted, but appreciated. A high-psychological-safety workplace does more than increase engagement; it fosters trust. Another key theory HR leaders can leverage to develop emotionally intelligent work environments.

EQ was formulated by Psychologist Daniel Goleman and includes self-awareness, self-regulation, motivation, empathy, and social skills. HR professionals with strong emotional intelligence can read between the lines more effectively, deal with conflicts, and see things from others' points of view. Likewise, developing emotional intelligence in leadership development courses also contributes to a culture of leading where leaders live with humility, humanity, and hope. And HR can also find value in employing standard models such as the Kübler-Ross Change Curve or Maslow's Hierarchy of Needs to simplify employee responses in times of upheaval or pressure. For example, the change curve lists individuals' emotional reactions as denial, anger, bargaining, depression, and acceptance, all of which are the stages that they are likely to face during times of large organizational changes. Understanding these stages can help HR create communication and support strategies that meet employees where they are emotionally, not where the company wishes they were. And there are practical tools like pulse surveys, stay interviews, and anonymous feedback mechanisms to collect real-time emotional data. These tools cannot be treated as stand-alone checkboxes, but as components of an ongoing conversation between leadership and the people who report to them.

When HR isn't just looking for trends in feedback, but for the emotions behind the feedback, frustration, hope, fear, and excitement, it can identify valuable insights for making meaningful moves. These emotional insights should then be communicated to leaders in a manner that encourages change rather than defensiveness. Employee resource groups (ERGs), mental health programs, and peer support networks are additional tactics that signify emotional support at an organization. These aren't mere skin-deep gestures. When employees feel that they and their struggles are recognized and supported, they are more likely to experience a sense of belonging. HR's challenge in this area is to drive these programs to be inclusive, accessible, and meet employee needs (versus just for the optics for leadership). Technology may provide some hints, but proceed with caution. Sentiment-analysis tools, powered by AI, can trawl company communication documents to pick up on morale shifts or stress trends. But, this type of surveillance needs to be conducted ethically and openly. Workers have to feel that HR wields its technology in support of them rather than spying on them. When implemented properly, these tools can also give HR an early warning when something signals the onset of burnout, disengagement, or conflict, before those situations get out of hand. But it will take the right leadership to get these tools and strategies to work. A tone of empathy and trust begins at the top. When leaders show that they are vulnerable themselves, can own up to errors, and truly listen to others, it creates a tone for the whole organization.

Leadership should not be considered a post; it should not just be restricted to decision-making, but it should be given the emotionally charged duty of leading your fellow people. It is HR's job to provide leaders with the necessary tools, along with constructive accountability when they miss the mark. Leadership matters a lot! Employees who trust their leaders are more engaged, innovative, and loyal. A leader who knows how to support someone who is overwhelmed, to celebrate small wins, to defuse tensions, can turn an environment that might otherwise be high pressure into one of growth and resilience. These small moments matter. What was said in a meeting fade, but how their manager made them feel stays. To make this all even more human, think about a recent college graduate who just landed a job at a company in the office for the first time and now, instead of trying to figure out the hard parts of a job, they are trying to figure out the invisible parts of a team's culture while working remotely. If HR and leadership have done the work to create emotional safety, this is a person who feels that they can ask questions, share ideas, and bring their whole self to work. They don't seem like a number in a spreadsheet. They feel seen. It's this kind of feeling of being known and being valued that turns employees into advocates for the company.

The symptoms of poor emotional intelligence are apparent in companies lacking emotional intelligence. Staff disengage, and collaboration suffers, innovation grinds to a standstill, and turnover goes up. The best strategy in the world can be easily derailed if we don't focus on the emotional health of our team. HR has a unique position and has the power to be the architect and the advocate of emotional culture through policy, programming, and presence. This is emotional labor, and it merits acknowledgment and respect. Greater support for HR's work if leaders are trained in coaching, active listening, and conflict resolution. Too often, those in leadership roles were elevated for technical ability, not people skills. One way that HR can narrow this chasm is by infusing emotional quotient into leadership training programs. Managers who are trained to see the whole person, rather than just the performance metrics, create teams with more resilience and adaptability. We can't overlook and devalue the emotional stories of these compassionate HR and people-person leaders who have made a great change in the lives of employees. One might say that a stay interview made them feel heard for the first time. Still, someone else might remember how their boss's flexibility during a family emergency served to bind the employee more tightly to the team.

Such stories are the beating heart of HR work. They're evidence that emotionally intelligent HR practices yield tangible, human results. Ultimately, managing the emotional terrain of an organization is not about fixing people or sidestepping discomfort. It is about creating spaces in which people feel free to be human. It's a place where emotions are not barriers to getting things done, but signals to be interpreted. HR can make it so, with the right tools and when working alongside the right leadership, that workplaces become communities of support, empathy, and purpose. Let this chapter be a reminder that while policies and metrics are important, it is people who bring the soul of the organization. And it's the emotional relations of them that make the work meaningful, permanently transformative.

One element that gets left out of the emotionally intelligent HR work is context. Emotions do not always make sense or appear logical. Life outside the office, from an illness or caregiving to financial stress or loss, comes with employees to work, whether we acknowledge it or not. By taking time to step back and understand the larger context of what is driving this behavior or mood shift, HR leaders act with empathy, rather than relying on assumptions to determine their next steps. Or think about the impact a manager can have when they notice an employee who's typically full of energy seeing their energy diminish. Instead of shunning the employee as disengaged or underperforming, a well-trained leader poses one straightforward, caring question: "Are you okay?" That moment of checking in, without agenda or judgment, can make a difference. It reinforces that moment of reminder to the worker that they are human, not just a body in a seat.

Another dimension to this job is HR as storytellers. It is a powerful skill to translate employees' experiences into stories that executives can digest and act on. Data may show that 30 percent of workers feel undervalued, but it is the story behind the data that prompts action.

One great story, well-told, can make that data come alive, and lead decision-makers to care, to listen, and to make a difference. What is more, mentoring relationships in an organizational context may provide formidable emotional support. HR can facilitate programs in which less experienced employees are matched with those more experienced and not just for transferring technical skills, but for reassurance, guidance, and a human connection. In stressful times, these relationships can serve as lifelines and bring resilience and continuity to the institution. HR can also nurture micro-moments of connection, short but deep interactions that build emotional safety. Thank you note, a kind word in a meeting, a sympathetic message after a long day: These gestures are free, but they make waves of goodwill. When leadership models and endorses these micro-moments across teams, they create a fabric of connection that keeps teams together during the hard times. And HR has to create room for emotional decompression. In a world where everyone's expected to be "on" all the time, designing structured moments for pause, mindfulness sessions, walking meetings, and even quiet lounges can help employees regulate their emotions. Emotional intelligence is woven into the very rhythm of the workday, where the pace of work respects the human need for rest and contemplation. And finally, none of that work is doable unless HR models it themselves. "If HR people are burned out, emotionally disconnected, or not emotionally attached, you can't create an emotionally aware culture. This is even more applicable to HR, who need the ability to retreat to safe spaces to reflect, process, and care for their own well-being too. Walking the walk allows everyone in HR to see that emotional intelligence isn't a trend; it's a value that comes to life from the core.

CHAPTER 5
PERSONAL NARRATIVES:
EMPLOYEES IN CRISIS AND THE
HEART OF HR AND LEADERSHIP

Every organization is made up of stories. Some are stories of triumph and growth, while others tell of struggle and hardship. When employees face crises, whether personal, family-related, or health-related, the impact ripples through their work lives and the people around them. These moments reveal not just the strength of individuals but also the true character of an organization, especially the role HR and leadership play in supporting their people.

Take, for example, Logia, a talented project manager who suddenly faced a family emergency. Overnight, her world was turned upside down, and the stress followed her into the workplace. Her usual vibrant energy dimmed, deadlines became mountains, and she started missing meetings. Her team noticed the change and felt the strain, unsure how to step in without crossing boundaries. The organization's response in such moments matters deeply; it can mean the difference between Logia feeling isolated or supported. Unfortunately, in many workplaces, employees like Logia suffer in silence. Sometimes, support systems are either too rigid or nonexistent, leaving individuals to manage crises on their own. When HR is reactive rather than proactive, these situations escalate, affecting morale and productivity. On the other hand, organizations that invest in compassionate HR policies and empathetic leadership create safety nets that help employees navigate tough times without feeling like their careers are at risk.

One critical support system is a flexible work policy. When Logia's manager offered her the option to work from home and adjust her hours, it wasn't just a convenience; it was a lifeline. That flexibility allowed her to tend to family needs while staying connected to her work and team. This kind of understanding sends a clear message: the organization values employees as whole people, not just as resources. Peer support networks also play a vital role. Sometimes, employees find the most comfort not from formal HR channels, but from colleagues who listen without judgment and offer small kindnesses. HR can help cultivate these networks by encouraging mentorship programs, affinity groups, or informal social circles that build camaraderie and resilience.

When people feel connected, they are better able to withstand personal crises without losing their footing professionally. The stories of employees who have navigated crises with support are inspiring. Consider Jamal, a customer service representative who experienced a mental health challenge that affected his focus and attendance. His HR team had recently launched a mental health initiative, complete with counseling services and wellness days. Jamal was hesitant at first, fearing stigma, but the open conversations led by his manager and HR reassured him that seeking help was not a weakness. Over time, Jamal regained his confidence, and his performance improved, showing how supportive environments can change lives.

However, the absence of support can be equally telling. Some employees face crises alone, their struggles masked by fear of judgment or job loss. This silence can fracture teams, increase turnover, and contribute to a toxic culture.

HR's challenge is to break down those barriers, normalizing conversations about mental health, caregiving, financial stress, and other external pressures that affect work life. HR and leadership must also recognize that taking care of themselves is fundamental to taking care of others. A leader who is overwhelmed or burned out cannot effectively guide their team through challenges. Self-care for leaders isn't a luxury; it's essential for sustainable leadership. When leaders model healthy boundaries, self-reflection, and openness about their own vulnerabilities, they create an environment where employees feel safe doing the same. This culture of care has a profound impact on retention. Employees who know their leaders see and support them as whole people are far more likely to stay loyal. They feel valued beyond their job description, and that loyalty translates into lower turnover rates and stronger team cohesion. Retention isn't just about compensation or benefits; it's about emotional connection and trust.

Leaders, You Cannot Give What You Do Not Have! You know that safety announcement they share during every flight: put on your own oxygen mask before the person beside you. Simple concept, but it is something in leadership that we often neglect. We care so much about our teams that we literally work ourselves to death trying to keep them safe, happy, and productive. So, we work late, take no lunch break, answer emails well into the night... while telling ourselves: "I am committed after all". But the reality of running empty does you and your team no favors. It takes a toll, and it sets an example that you most likely do not want them to learn. Your Energy Is Their Energy. Did you ever perceive how the general time of a social event can change from when you enter the room? Your team will feel it the moment you walk through that door, stressed, rushed, or with nothing left in the tank. Likewise, if you show up relaxed, centered, and there with them in the moment, it creates space for your team to relax in their bodies as well, which is where optimal learning happens. Leadership is a mirror. Your team follows what they see in you. If you treat self-care as optional, they will too. If you stand up for yourself, so can they.

The Mixed Message Trap

We are all, (me included) are guilty, don't work late guys (I say as I send an email at 8 pm). You might be thinking that this guy will just take a rain check and everything will be fine, but from their perspective, they hear a different message: "My boss is working, so I should be too!"

The fear of being too committed is clear. It is not what you mean, but what they are feeling. If you want your employees to value their time, make sure that you do too.

Protect their time by protecting yours. One of the easiest acts of care in leadership. Stop sending after-hours emails. Draft them if you must but schedule their send so that it shows up during business hours. Or make it clear in the subject line that it can wait. When you care for your boundaries, you give your team permission to care for them. That's how you build a culture in which people can unplug without guilt. Self-care doesn't have to be complicated. It's not about week-long spa days; it's about moments that keep you focused and kind, two things your team desperately needs from you. Real breaks, a nourishing meal, moving your body, sleeping, a life outside of work *the leader they'll remember. Your team may not remember all your decisions in 10 years, but they will recall the way you make them feel: valued, supported, and secure enough to care for themselves. And the best part? Self-care helps you become the leader you aspire to be. You'll have the patience to listen, the strength to lead, and the courage to make the right decision for your people. So, pause for a moment. Close your laptop on time. Go out and do something. You're not leaving leadership behind; you're the only way to keep leading.

Leader's Self-Care Promise

I promise to care for myself so I can care for my team.

- I will protect my health, rest, and energy so I can show up fully for the people who count on me.
- I will take my breaks and my time off because recovery makes me a stronger, more present leader.
- I will model the balance I want my team to have because what I do matters more than what I say.
- I will respect my own time and theirs by avoiding after-hours requests unless it's truly urgent.
- I will use my vacation without guilt and encourage my team to do the same.
- I will bring the best version of myself to work each day, not the most exhausting.
- I will remember that leadership is not about how much I give up, but how well I lift others up.

When I take care of myself, I lead with clarity, patience, and heart, and that's the Leader my team deserves.

Looking ahead, the role of HR and leadership is to shape a future where empathy and support are baked into the organization's DNA. It's about creating policies that are flexible, benefits that are meaningful, and leadership programs that develop emotional intelligence. This approach doesn't just protect employees, it drives growth. Organizations that prioritize well-being innovate faster, adapt better, and outperform competitors. There's also a financial reality tied to this human approach. When employees are supported through crises, organizations reduce costs related to absenteeism, errors, and turnover. The investment in wellness programs, training, and flexible work pays dividends in productivity and morale. Leadership and HR, therefore, are not only caretakers of people but stewards of organizational sustainability.

Beyond policy and programs, HR plays a crucial storytelling role, translating personal narratives into organizational learning. Sharing anonymized stories of resilience and recovery helps humanize data and motivate leadership to act with heart. It reminds everyone that behind every metric is a person with challenges and potential. Ultimately, Chapter 5 underscores a powerful truth: organizations succeed when their people thrive. The personal crises employees face do not exist in a vacuum; they shape how work gets done and how teams connect. HR and leadership must step into these stories with empathy, tools, and a commitment to care, creating workplaces where people feel truly supported, empowered, and valued.

CHAPTER 6
CRISIS MANAGEMENT WITH HEART: HOW HR CAN RESPOND WITH SENSITIVITY AND STRATEGY

Crisis is, and always will be, the workplace. Whether it's a personal tragedy, a health emergency, a natural disaster, or a large-scale organizational disruption, employees will experience times when their world feels shaky. HR's role in such moments is much broader than that of enforcing policy and procedure; it is about reaching the emotional core of what it means to work in an environment that recognizes and supports you. The lessons of crisis are that the effective managers first empathize and then prepare. HR is usually on the spot when people go through things that are difficult. The most crucial thing in those moments isn't having all the answers, but showing up, listening, and responding. Tone, above all,   and simply listening and wanting to help, even if there aren't easy answers, can make all the difference to someone whose life has just changed drastically.

But waiting for a crisis is not the answer. Pre-emptive crisis management is putting systems in place before employees demand them. This could be wellness check-ins, mental health resources, or helping train managers to see early warning signs. HR needs to get more preventive, just as any good health professional is more focused on wellness than treatment. One of the easiest and most effective things HR can do is develop relationships. Workers are also much more likely to talk about their struggles or ask for help if they feel safe doing so. But psychological safety doesn't come from one-time HR memos; it comes from sustained trust, built through transparent communication and follow-through. When people feel HR has their back, they talk.

In order to spot employees in need before it's too late, HR has the opportunity to help create a culture that destigmatizes the act of seeking help. This starts with leadership. By sharing their individual stories and experiences of navigating grief, illness, or burnout, a director sends a signal to the team that vulnerability isn't a liability. It becomes acceptable, even courageous, to say, "I'm not okay right now." Regular check-ins with employees can also lend a hand in early detection. It's not all or nothing. Not every conversation has to be official. A five-minute chat at someone's desk, or a brief message that says, "Hey, you've seemed off lately, everything okay?" may be the beginning of an essential intervention. HR, in turn, needs to enable managers to have these conversations and provide the tools to do so with sensitivity and confidentiality.

Another "smart" strategy involves including emotional well-being questions on engagement surveys. By knowing what to ask, not just in terms of job satisfaction but in assessing one's level of stress, support systems, and psychological safety, HR can collect data that demonstrates to leadership emerging trends and vulnerable areas before they become crises. Another game-changer can be building an internal "Crisis Response Toolkit." These might take the form of short guidelines for managers, templates for crisis communication, lists of resources for mental health or financial assistance, and even checklists for follow-up care. When everything feels out of control, knowing exactly what you need to do next will calm your body from panic and put structure into chaos. Training is essential.

Both HR staff and people managers should be trained in how to respond to crises, prevent and address trauma, and connect employees to resources. Training to have empathy should address role-playing in the skill, how to respond to crying people, how to talk to employees when a loved one has died, and how to react when you learn that your employee is a victim of domestic violence. It is a difficult conversation; we are not there yet. Of course, confidentiality is of the essence. There's nothing that erodes trust more quickly than gossip or violation of privacy. HR also needs to be razor clear regarding what stays confidential and what is so serious it gets escalated (eg, safety threats). These limits have to be explained to employees kindly but firmly, so that when they step forward, they understand what to expect. Collaborating with outside experts is another smart play. HR should not aim to be a therapist, a lawyer, or a financial adviser. Rather, they are encouraged to create a chain of trusted referrals, employee assistance programs (EAPs), therapists,   legal resources, crisis hotlines, and so on. Because of these partnerships, employees can call on expertise when they need it most. In times of crisis, flexibility is compassion. Whether that's providing remote work, adjusted deadlines, extended leave, or a temporary reassignment, HR can have a tremendous effect by asking the simple question: "What would make you feel supported right now?" Not one size fits all,   and small adjustments can make all the difference.

The tone and phraseology during a crisis also count. Make your HR communications clear, calm, and human instead of confusing your employees. Make your HR communications precise, clear, calm, and human. Steer clear of corporate speak and empty buzzwords. We're here for you, and we'll get through this together goes a long way, whereas "See policy

#48.1 for crisis protocol" falls flat as a pancake. One such aspect is the post-crisis response. After the initial shock subsides, many employees continue fighting silently. HR needs to schedule follow-up check-ins, not just once but over time, to help ensure that recovery is continuing. Healing is not a straight line, and people often require a variety of kinds of support as they progress.

HR also needs to take care of its own team. Serving as a caregiver in the workplace is exhausting, too, where HR employees are on the hook for the emotional fallout from others' crises. Who helps HR when HR needs help?

In times of upheaval, HR professionals are often the first line of defense for an organization; they are its peacemakers. And at the same time, HR must be responsible for setting a tone and leading by example in a crisis. That's a big job. HR professionals' debut with an overview of the role. But under the policies and rules is always a human heart; that heart is chunky and full of flesh.HR doesn't just help people. Sometimes it helps people too much. With the weight of the world on their shoulders, it can be hard for HR practitioners to remember that they have only two shoulders. This chapter pipes out a reminder: HR is not alone. There are people in this world your branch can turn to for help and hope. Don't forget that, even though you may be hunkering down under fire.

The Emotional Toll on HR: HR often handles the repercussions of layoffs, sexual harassment inquiries, and when employees are victimized. As the July/August 2012 edition of the Harvard Business Review noted, the mental health of employees, including HR, is under increasing pressure. In the age of digital revolution, world economic uncertainty, and new political geography, what effect will these things have on our minds?

You Also Deserve Support. Support for HR needs to be routine, contiguous, and sympathetic. Here are a few suggestions for HR professionals who have lost their way—to find help even if they are not in charge:

Employee Assistance Programs (EAPs) offer Confidential counseling and resources for stress, anxiety, depression, and family conflicts, becoming more important with every year that flies. These programs are not just for "other employees" any longer; HR needs them, too.

Peer Networks and HR Communities Local HR communities, HR Houston, and Web boards function like secret places where HR professionals can let off steam and be frank. These communities remind HR that they, too, have a support group.

Mental Health Advocacy The Harvard Business Review suggests that leaders - including HR- look at mental health from a holistic stance. A candid discussion of your own problems can breed trust and purity in the workplace.

Reflective Practices HRZone and Forbes Magazine suggest that HR practitioners develop reflective and responsible examination practices as well as supervision. These help to create a space for their own reflection, growth, and eventual healing.

When HR Gets It Wrong, every now and then mistakes will occur, rules bent, truths chafed. When HR comes to a cropper, it's not so much a collapse as it is a time for healing.

If you're not in charge, but you can see there's been a mistake:

Carefully document: Essential details should be collected, not to accuse but instead to clarify. Express sensitive emotion: Speak with HR about their problems in a disinterested and curious tone. Elevate with respect: Use official avenues of approach for any comments made or difficulties you experience and keep looking for a solution -not vengeance.

A Message to Every HR Professional: You are not simply the job you perform. You are an individual.

You have the right to ask for help. You have the right to feel overwhelmed. You have the right to be supported.

You are not alone.

Let this chapter serve as a reminder: HR is deserving of care, compassion, and community. You're not only the one who serves you but are also worth helping.

Check-ins and access to therapy and team-based help make it less likely that those who care for everyone else will burn themselves out. Beyond the emotional part, there is another strategic advantage of compassionate crisis management. It's a chance for organizations to prove themselves to their people at a critical time and create loyalty when it's needed most, which, ideally, is the job description of companies in the first place. You remember how you were treated when you were at your lowest. A kind response today could result in a long-term commitment tomorrow. How do you minimize turnover and maximize retention when, at the end of the day, it tends to be these moments? When employees feel cared for and supported in difficult times, they are much more likely to stay, speak well of the organization, and invest in its future.

Responding to the crisis is not only a moral obligation, but it's a retention strategy. And, done well, crisis response can be an extension of a company's brand. A reputation for prioritizing its employees during life's most challenging periods and circumstances can help win talent, boost its standing in a community, and distinguish a business in competitive markets. It sends the signal that this isn't only a workplace, but a human place. The future of hard management in HR is data-informed yet heart-driven. Listening to people's stories, tracking trends, and tweaking strategies positions HR to guide organizations gracefully and resiliently through the unknown. And as the pandemic became more entwined with more and different challenges, from economic distress to social unrest, organizations that place humanity at the center of their response will be the ones that most succeed. In the end, it's all just this: Crisis doesn't stand down for policy. It comes a-knocking at the door unannounced. The difference between good organizations and bad ones is not whether they make mistakes, good organizations do; it's whether they are willing to recognize their mistakes and learn from them. And at its best, HR has the potential to transform instances of harm into sources of support, healing, and, ultimately, trust.

CHAPTER 7
BEYOND THE SURFACE

Work is not just where we go to get a paycheck, though in many cases, that's exactly what it starts out as. We don't work, most of us, because we want to. We're working because we need to. We have mouths to feed, rent or mortgages to pay, and obligations that do not include taking days off. However, in the blur of emails, meetings, and never-ending to-do lists, we somehow forget that behind every job title is a human being. A person with a story. I've written this book because I know what can happen when that truth is forgotten. I have watched leaders make assumptions without context, and I have watched employees lose faith because they felt unseen. This book, Beyond the Surface: Navigating Human Resources with Compassion and Insight, is my heart on paper. That is my hope, my plea, my prayer that we start showing up differently. That we start to see one another, truly see one another, below the surface.

Each chapter leading up to this one was a part of that journey. We've delved into the structures, the systems, and the strategies that form HR, but at the heart of it, human resources is just that: human. It's about people. And people are beautifully messy, flawed, and resilient. If we want to lead well, support well, or just work well with others, we have to recognize that. This is the chapter that I want lingering with you long after you've closed the book. I want this to be the page you return to when your patience is short or your assumptions are loud. This is your reminder. This is our reset. Because here's the reality: everyone is dealing with something. Everyone. The colleague who appears disengaged might be tending to a sick parent. The staff member who's been late three times this week may be trying to decide between buying gas for their car and buying groceries. The leader who comes off as aloof may be battling silent anxiety. And we don't always get the details.

But we do get to decide how we show up. Grace is not a weakness. Compassion isn't inefficiency. Kindness is not a liability. These are the things that create trust, loyalty, and connection, and that create the place that people want to stay and work in. So, how do we do it? How can we move from judgment to curiosity? From frustration to empathy? From managing to leading? It starts with presence. With noticing. By asking, "Are you okay?" and actually meaning it. By slowing down long enough to learn, not just react. We all have bad days, and we all need someone to believe in us on those days. If you're a leader, your job isn't just to achieve results; it's to create an environment where others can be successful, even on bad days. If you work for an organization, your job is not simply to work there; it's to be a part of a culture that makes everyone better. We're all responsible for the energy we bring into a room. We're all responsible for how we treat one another.

In humanizing the workplace, we breed belonging. We make safety, and these are the things that open up creativity, dedication, and courage. Until then, let's not wait until we're in a crisis to care. We need to not wait for someone to break down before we acknowledge their load. Let's check in early. Let's check in often. Let's build work cultures where people are held in esteem, even when they're fighting to get by. Because we've all struggled. I've struggled. There have been days I've sat in the car and cried before entering the office, days I've sat in meetings, straining to smile, when the weight on my heart nearly crushed me. And I know I'm not the only one. You've been there too. So let this be your permission slip chapter to feel, to care, to lead with heart. Make it your game plan to infuse compassion into policy, empathy into feedback, and grace into goals. Here's what I've found: Professional does not mean unfriendly. Efficiency is not the same as a lack of warmth. The very best leaders I have the privilege to know have the names, notice the little things, and say "thank you" like they mean it. The greatest teams I've witnessed are those in which you can be honest and still be safe. You don't need a title to lead with empathy. You only need to be brave enough to say it out loud.

When I wrote this book, I certainly didn't write it only for HR professionals. I was writing it for everyone who's been misunderstood at work. And I'm aware that's pretty much all of us. For everyone who just needs one more chance. For the folks who keep coming back each day, even when it's impossible. For the leaders doing the best they can, most of the time, they feel they're failing. I hope every desk, every breakroom, gets a copy of this book. I hope it makes us remember that we are all in this together. That we are all just human, doing the best we can, holding stories we haven't even told. I want you to read this book and think about the way you arrive. Consider your tone in emails. Your patience in meetings. Your reaction to somebody fumbling the ball. Do you lead with curiosity? Or with criticism? Make grace your go-to. Make empathy your reflex. Create room for humans to be human.

Beyond the Surface Pulse Check
(Your weekly guide to connection in isolation)
- Did I take the best view of someone today?
- Did I meet a challenge with compassion?
- Did I allow space for someone to be honest or vulnerable?
- Did I thank someone on my team?
- Did I extend grace, especially when grace wasn't earned?
- Did I ask, "Are you okay?" and truly mean it?
- Did I think before I told others what to say or do?
- Did I treat people as people, not just as roles or job titles?
- Did I bring good vibes into my space?
- Would I help somebody feel seen today?

Make a paste-up of this list and stick it somewhere you see regularly, your desk, your notebook, your phone. Use it to pause and consider each week. Be honest with yourself. When you do fall short, don't dwell on it; learn, adapt, and go again.

Your Action Plan

Here's how to put this strategy into action. Select one of these practices to try this week. Whether it's listening more or giving grace. Choose only one, so it's manageable.

- Set a daily reminder. A friendly reminder or buzzer that tells you to visit your selected focus.
- Journal briefly. Keep a running list at the end of each day of at least one moment where you succeeded and one where you feel you fell short.
- Ask for feedback. Ask a trusted colleague or friend to offer an honest perspective on how you're showing up.
- Celebrate small wins. It may be in yourself or in someone else, but when you see progress, then you say something, or you write it down.
- Practice self-compassion. Change isn't instant. If you slip, remind yourself why this is important and get back on track.
- Share the pulse check. Ask your team or friends to join you. Compassion multiplies when we create it together.
- Make time for connection. Whether it's a simple check-in, a genuine thank you, or even a listening ear, make room for some real human interaction.
- Reflect monthly. At the end of every month, look back over your journal and feedback. What patterns do you see? Where are you flourishing? What needs more care?
- Remember your commitment. Revisit this strategy often. Let it remind you why niceness at work isn't just nice, it's necessary.

It's not about being perfect. It's about being present. Being real. Deciding to care, especially when it's hard. For when we look past the surface, past the deadlines, past the roles, the thing we are looking for lies at the heart of work itself: People. People with stories, with struggles, with hopes, with dreams. If this helps you pause, listen, or take it down a notch once, the work is already having its effect right here. So, here's to leading from the heart. Here's to showing up as something more, not only as professionals but as human beings that matter. The world of work can seem oppressive, but together we can lighten it. It's what's beneath the surface that makes the magic.

From Insight to Action

Embedding Compassionate Leadership in Organizational Culture

As we close the pages of *Beyond the Surface*, it becomes clear that this book is not just a reflection; it is a call to action. The journey through each chapter has revealed a powerful truth: human resources is not merely a department; it is the emotional and ethical compass of an organization. It is where policy meets people, and where leadership must be rooted in empathy, accountability, and courage.

Key Concepts Recap

The foundation of leadership is empathy, emotional intelligence, and a sense of justice.

1. Leaders are far more than mere decision makers; they are also the culture shapers who set the tone for how people feel and how they perform when completing tasks.
2. Psychological Safety When people feel safe to speak their minds, a culture of innovation and accountability can flourish.
3. Transparent Communication Trust is earned through honesty. Good leaders articulate the 'why' and operate a what we know, what we don't framework.
4. Employee Well-being Support is integral to supporting the whole person — including mental health, personal challenges, and flexibility in how work can be done now digitally. Open to work leaders must normalize learning by failing fast, then moving on from it.
5. Crisis Management with Heart. The pragmatic approach is to deal with it in advance rather than in a knee-jerk reaction. In other words, a blend of empathy combined with your strategic thinking creates loyalty, resilience, and trust over the long haul.
6. Inclusive Culture: These are non-negotiables to me when it comes to equity, diversity, and belonging. All employees deserve to be seen (observations), heard (listening), and valued (respect)all the time.

7. Accountability and Growth Cam says that leaders need to walk the walk when it comes to accountability, be open to feedback, and always be learning. Everyone is responsible for growth, and that's what drives success.

Why These Concepts Matter

For employees and leaders, these principles are a map for an ever-growing impact. They build trust, inspiration, and so much more... They make for a place where all those high-potential employees you have hired cannot just survive but also thrive. Compassionate leadership is not soft; it is strategic. The result is a happier and more committed workforce that turns up, stays put, and exceeds figures. To Organizations – These are principles of sustained success. Emotionally intelligent, transparent, and well-being-driven organizations outperform their competitors, attract top talent, retain key skills, and build adaptive company cultures that last.

Leadership Assessment Tool

■ Key Concepts Recap

- Human-Centered Leadership – Lead with empathy, fairness, and emotional intelligence.

- Psychological Safety – Build an environment where team members feel safe to speak openly.

- Transparent Communication – Foster trust by sharing the "why" behind decisions.

- Employee Well-being – Support the whole person, both inside and outside of work.

- Crisis Management with Heart – Combine compassion with strategic, clear actions.

- Inclusive Culture – Seek equity and welcome diverse perspectives.

- Accountability and Growth – Embrace feedback, self-reflection, and continuous improvement.

■ Leadership Self-Assessment

Instructions: Rate yourself on each statement from 1 (Rarely) to 5 (Consistently).

#	Statement	Score (1–5)
1	I lead with empathy and consider the emotional needs of my team.	
2	I create a psychologically safe environment.	
3	I communicate transparently and explain the "why."	
4	I support employee well-being through flexibility and understanding.	
5	I respond to crises with compassion and clear action plans.	
6	I actively seek and value diverse perspectives.	
7	I hold myself accountable and welcome feedback.	

Scoring Guide:
07–14 □ Growth Opportunity
Focus on strengthening foundational leadership skills.

15–24 □ Emerging Leader
Build consistency across leadership practices.

25–35 □ Compassionate Leader
You model human-centered leadership.

■ Action Plan for Growth

- Choose one area to focus on each month.
- Set a specific, measurable goal (e.g., 'Hold weekly check-ins').
- Reflect weekly using the Pulse Check from chapter seven.
- Seek feedback from peers, mentors, or direct reports.
- Celebrate progress and adjust as needed.

Personal Leadership Growth Plan

Use this space to outline your monthly leadership focus, goals, and progress notes.

Month	Focus Area	Goal	Reflection Notes

References

Articles from Health Psychology Research are provided here courtesy of **Open Medical Publishing**
Impact of Toxic Leadership on Employee Performance - PMC (nih.gov)

1. Akca M. The Impact of Toxic Leadership on Intention to Leave of Employees. International Journal of Economics, Business and Management Research. 2017;1(04):285-298.
2. Paltu A, Brouwers M. Toxic Leadership: Effects on Job Satisfaction, Commitment, Turnover Intention and Organisational Culture within the South African Manufacturing Industry. SA j hum resour manag. 2020;18:1-11. doi:10.4102/sajhrm.v18i0.1338
3. Vreja LO, Balan S, Bosca LC. An Evolutionary Perspective on Toxic Leadership. Management and Economics Review. 2016;1(2):217-228.
4. Bhandarker A, Rai S. Toxic Leadership: Emotional Distress and Coping Strategy. IJOTB. 2019;22(1):65-78. doi:10.1108/ijotb-03-2018-0027
5. Kurtulmuş BE. Toxic Leadership and Workplace Bullying: The Role of Followers and Possible Coping Strategies. In: The Palgrave Handbook of Workplace Well-Being; 2020:1-20.
6. Toropova A, Myrberg E, Johansson S. Teacher Job Satisfaction: The Importance of School Working Conditions and Teacher Characteristics. Educational Review. 2020;73(1):1-27.
7. Dhamija P, Gupta S, Bag S. Measuring of Job Satisfaction: The Use of Quality of Work Life Factors.

BIJ. 2019;26(3):871-892. doi:10.1108/bij-06-2018-0155

8. Hoboubi N, Choobineh A, Kamari Ghanavati F, Keshavarzi S, Akbar Hosseini A. The Impact of Job Stress and Job Satisfaction on Workforce Productivity in an Iranian Petrochemical Industry. Safety and Health at Work. 2017;8(1):67-71. doi:10.1016/j.shaw.2016.07.002 [PMC free article] [PubMed]

9. Chandani A, Mehta M, Mall A, Khokhar V. Employee Engagement: A Review Paper on Factors Affecting Employee Engagement. Indian Journal of Science and Technology. 2016;9(15). doi:10.17485/ijst/2016/v9i15/92145

10. Rizal M, Idrus MS, Mintarti R. Effect of Compensation on Motivation, Organizational Commitment and Employee Performance (Studies at Local Revenue Management in Kendari City). International Journal of Business and Management Invention. 3(2):2319-8028.

11. Hee OC et al. Exploring the Impact of Communication on Employee Performance. International Journal of Recent Technology and Engineering. 2019;8(3S2):654-658.

12. Matos K, O'Neill OM, Lei X. Toxic Leadership and the Masculinity Contest Culture: How "Win or Die" Cultures Breed Abusive Leadership. Journal of Social Issues. 2018;74(3):500-528. doi:10.1111/josi.12284

13. Milosevic I, Maric S, Lončar D. Defeating the Toxic Boss: The Nature of Toxic Leadership and the Role of Followers. Journal of Leadership and Organizational Studies. 27(2):1-21.

14. Al Mehrzi N, Singh SK. Competing through Employee Engagement: A Proposed Framework. International

Journal of Productivity and Performance Management. 2016;65(6):831-843. doi:10.1108/ijppm-02-2016-0037

Sources

https://www.forbes.com/advisor/business/hr-statistics-trends/#sources_section

- Harvard Business Review
- Recruiting Daily
- LinkedIn
- Forbes
- Bureau of Labor Statistics
- Work Institute
- Benefit News
- Forbes Advisor
- SHRM
- Wall Street Journal

ABOUT THE AUTHOR

Angela Rasheed-Stephens is a compassionate leader, a seasoned human resources professional, and a passionate advocate for equity and emotional intelligence in the workplace. With over two decades of experience navigating complex organizational dynamics, Angela brings a deeply personal and transformative approach to HR leadership-one grounded in empathy, transparency, and accountability.

Throughout her career, she has guided individuals and institutions through moments of crisis, cultural change, and leadership restructuring. Her insights are shaped not just by policy, but by people-their stories, struggles, and silent battles often hidden behind job titles and expectations.

Angela is a sought-after speaker, trainer, and advisor on issues related to organizational culture, mental health in the workplace, and leadership development. *Beyond the Surface* is her debut book, born from years of hard-earned wisdom and a firm belief that compassion is the true currency of impactful leadership.

She resides in Texas, where she continues to mentor professionals and champions in inclusive, people-first workplaces.

www.ingramcontent.com/pod-product-compliance
Lightning Source LLC
Chambersburg PA
CBHW070458130626
46555CB00003B/1061